D0173123

The
Sophisticated
Alcoholic

The
Sophisticated
Alcoholic

David Allen

BOOKS

Winchester, UK
Washington, USA

First published by O-Books, 2011
O-Books is an imprint of John Hunt Publishing Ltd., Laurel House, Station Approach,
Alresford, Hants, SO24 9JH, UK
office1@o-books.net
www.o-books.com

For distributor details and how to order please visit the 'Ordering' section on our website.

Text copyright: David Allen 2010

ISBN: 978 1 84694 522 9

All rights reserved. Except for brief quotations in critical articles or reviews, no part of
this book may be reproduced in any manner without prior written permission from
the publishers.

The rights of David Allen as author have been asserted in accordance with the Copyright, Designs
and Patents Act 1988.

A CIP catalogue record for this book is available from the British Library.

Design: Stuart Davies

Printed in the UK by CPI Antony Rowe
Printed in the USA by Offset Paperback Mfrs, Inc

We operate a distinctive and ethical publishing philosophy in all
areas of our business, from our global network of authors to
production and worldwide distribution.

CONTENTS

Dedication

Ever since I can remember I've wanted security and stability in my life. Whether through fortune or desire, things seem to have turned out just as I had hoped. Sandra, my wife since 1969, has always loved me when, perhaps, I didn't deserve that. We have two sons of whom I am immensely proud who now both have families of their own and so another generation grows.

This book has come to fruition because of this stability and support, even through the drinking years. For that reason I dedicate it to my family. It is the strength I draw from them that underpins my life and work.

Acknowledgement

Dr James Kustow, Contributor and Editor

I truly thank my friend and colleague Dr James Kustow for his considerable help in making this manuscript as readable and accurate as it is. He has pored over every word making helpful suggestions and alterations at every point so that my message is clear and understandable.

We thought it important to set the scene into which this new and exciting approach emerges. In an introductory chapter he explains how alcohol misuse is conceptualized clinically, explores the complex issue of causation and briefly overviews current mainstream treatment approaches. Through a scientific yet exploratory stance, he opens the path for new ideas to emerge as he talks frankly about his experience of the limitations of some aspects of the mainstream approach to alcohol addiction. His therapeutic insights, especially in the skilled use of EFT[1], have added richness through his editing.

Dr Kustow is a full time NHS Psychiatrist working in London. Following his basic medical training and a period of a few years working as a regular hospital doctor, he trained in General Adult Psychiatry in a number of the leading London teaching hospitals, achieving his Membership of the Royal College in 2006. He has recently reached Consultant Psychiatrist level.

His interests include psychological trauma (more specifically the processing of unresolved traumatic memory using body-focused psychotherapeutic techniques) and impulse control disorders, in particular Adult ADHD. He also has extensive experience and a formal endorsement in Liaison (or General Hospital) Psychiatry, the clinical interface between the mind and body.

He has trained in a number of psychotherapeutic approaches including EMDR (Adv), EFT (Adv), TFT, PEP and Hypnotherapy and he sees a small number of clients for private psychotherapy using an integrated model, combining the complexity and depth of traditional psychoanalytic thinking with the potency of some of these new body-based, memory processing techniques.

Dr Kustow is the founder of the 'Marrow' charity which is affiliated to the Anthony Nolan Trust. Marrow trains medical students in every medical school in the United Kingdom, and in medical schools in over 10 other countries, to run regular bone marrow donor recruitment clinics for all of the other university students on campus. The charity provides over a third of UK donors and raises over £50,000 a year.

Foreword

Ed Mitchell

I was a successful television presenter and journalist yet as a result of my addiction to alcohol I lost everything – my job, my house, my marriage, my driving license – and ended up bankrupt and sleeping rough. I was close to losing life itself.

Through a series of very unusual, fortunate and public events in 2007, I was able to get on the path to recovery[2], since then my whole perception of alcohol has fundamentally changed. Alcohol is still absolutely everywhere (literally in my case – my flat is above an off-license), but because of that radical change in my attitude, it is now an irrelevance.

The whole experience has shown me several things: that alcohol addiction can be beaten, that I was not alone, that life is so much happier without addiction, and that *there are many routes to recovery.*

Those many paths to recovery include, among others, the 12-Step approach of Alcoholics Anonymous[3] and the newer versions of Smart Recovery, Intuitive Recovery, Rational Recovery, Human Givens and the whole field of cognitive behavioral therapy.

Many books covering these methods have been written and dozens of inspiring personal stories have been told, but very little had been said about the effects of our belief system in starting and sustaining a dependency upon alcohol. This is where *The Sophisticated Alcoholic* fills a gap.

David Allen is a hypnotherapist and an energy therapist and works with these tools to help people change the way they think and behave with alcohol. This book is about how you can do this for yourself.

The first step to overcoming alcohol addiction is a real desire to change – but that can't be just a superficial wanting to change. David's approach recognizes that our fundamental beliefs are held at the subconscious level and that to achieve permanent change, they have to be changed at that level as well, This approach gives us the 'how to', it provides the explanations, gives us the tools, and provides support.

For me, breaking the chemical bond to alcohol was the first step – painful but short. The second was a longer process of reversing 40 years of habitual drink-thinking. The third step was, and is, by far the most rewarding – opening up the spiritual dimension, and this is where the real enjoyment begins.

This groundbreaking work offers an understanding of the how the brain, mind and soul can work in harmony to bring tranquility into a troubled life and eliminate the need for damaging behavior.

One of the etymological roots of the word 'sophisticated' is the Greek for 'wise person'. The wisdom I hope I have gained through the experience of alcohol addiction and recovery is that being a slave to a chemical makes life very dark and small – a tragedy when life is actually so full of light, love and happiness.

You don't have to end up sleeping rough to discover that simple truth. If you think you might have a problem or know someone who has, or are just interested in this fascinating subject – reading this will provide valuable help and is a real insight into why you drink too much and how you can change that forever.

Ed Mitchell

Part 1 - Cause and effect

Chapter I

Introduction

I write this book from the somewhat unusual perspective of being an ex-abuser of alcohol as well as a therapist. I haven't used the word 'alcoholic', although that might well be true, but I do use the word 'ex' to signify that it isn't just the fact that I don't drink alcohol to excess any more, but that it is a problem resolved. I don't mean that I never touch alcohol and neither am I afraid of it. As I no longer have the same relationship with this powerful drug I can, and do sometimes drink. I could even drink enough of it to become drunk though that hasn't happened since this change came about.

The reason is simple, it no longer holds the importance it once did and the need to use it in the quantities and with the regularity I once did, has collapsed.

Going downhill

I recall those times walking down the hill late on a Friday night returning home from my local pub in the quiet of the early morning hours. I would just amble along with that regular adjustment in the step that inebriation often requires in order to remain balanced. Ten minutes later I'm tucked up in bed. Ten minutes and two seconds later I'm dead to the world.

This would happen every Friday night and sometimes on a Wednesday and Thursday too, but always on Friday night. Quite often a friend would join me on this walk down the hill to my home and, egging each other on, we would invariable crack open another bottle of wine and continue the usually highly animated discussion until the sobering prospect of a new day drew proceedings to a close.

Saturdays and Sundays created their own separate routines in a more family-orientated and social environment. The consistent factor would always, however, be the alcohol.

The pub was a good place and it engendered a warm feeling of belonging. In the days of 11pm closing, it was reassuring to be a part of the select group to be allowed to remain for a while longer – the joys of the 'lock-in'. Doors bolted and curtains drawn, the gentlemanly banter and alcohol consumption continued into the early hours.

I understand now that a deeply subconscious part of my mind had developed a routine, almost a ritual, centered on alcohol, without me consciously agreeing to it; an ingrained set of rules that managed and organized my drinking habit. At that time my internal chatter would tell me that these allocated drinking slots were opportunities to *meet with friends* and *unwind* and *what's wrong with that?*

I drank in a disciplined way and rarely allowed the effects of it to interfere with other important duties that had to be performed. Due to the close management and normalization of my alcohol consumption and the fact that I attempted to lead a broader and more varied life, I could remain content in the belief that I was just a person who enjoyed *the odd drink.* There was *nothing to worry about.* I didn't let it affect my work or my other non-drinking activities and I didn't drive when I was drinking (mostly), so all in all, it fitted quite nicely into my self-excusing vision of a well ordered and satisfying existence. The reality, however, wasn't quite like that.

Although I saw my drinking as ordered and managed, others didn't take the same view. When I had been drinking heavily my behavior left something to be desired and typically in my state of overt inebriation I failed to see, until many years later, how unpleasantly I was acting.

Many years ago I was a student at a college in Kent, in South East England. My employer at the time, the energy supplier

British Gas, had a policy of allowing employees time off work for educational improvement. Having worked for them for a while, I took advantage of that opportunity and spent some five years attending college in an attempt to better myself.

The course was a Diploma in Management Studies and as well as the regular classes there were also residential weekends devoted to personal and group study where we were encouraged to focus all our attention on the tasks set and the lectures delivered without the distraction of normal weekend activities.

Any formal work that got done during these seminars would have been quite incidental. Within the class a group was quickly established whose main objective became to consume as much alcohol as possible. There were four of us for whom this event was seen purely as an escape from responsibility and a welcome opportunity to let down the hair that we all still had back then. Most of the rest of the class seemed more circumspect, but we didn't care. With the arrogance of youth we assumed that we could do the minimum study between drinking and still achieve a pass grade.

One of the locations for these weekend trips was the Nayland Rock Hotel in Margate. This was an uninspiring place where we huddled round the jukebox trying to keep warm from the lights inside. It was freezing cold but the bar was open and stayed open until around four in the morning. So, all in all, we were quite content with the place.

On the second visit, despite the accommodating bar staff, we had still brought considerable alcohol reinforcements which, as it happened, proved necessary when the bar closed early and we were in no mood to stop the festivities. After the bar had closed the four of us decided to head back to my room for more drinks from the reserve stock we had brought along.

Before leaving for the room I went to the toilet and followed along just a few minutes later. When I knocked on the door there was no reply. I knocked again, still no reply. Clearly, I concluded, they were keeping quiet and constructing some amusement at my expense. I was not to be outdone. I remembered that when I had checked-in earlier the door to my room wasn't as secure as it might have been. Even when locked it seemed loose so I concluded that a gentle nudge might open it. I kicked the door close to the lock and in my inebriated condition, misjudged it. Not only did the door open but the frame splintered all the way round with half of it falling into the room. The door swung open rather quickly, collided with whatever stood in its path, then bounced back to an almost closed position. Strangely, this seemed quite reasonable to me at the time.

As I entered the room and switched on the lights I was surprised to find a strange little ginger haired man sat bolt upright in bed with the covers pulled up to his chin. He was clearly as surprised to see me as I was him. Checking the door number I realized that stupidly I had come to the wrong floor. Giggling to myself, I stumbled back to my own room mindlessly leaving his door ajar, content in the conviction that this was a perfectly reasonable mistake to make. By the time I'd returned and rejoined the group I had completely forgotten the event had even happened. Despite the unusual and destructive nature of the uninvited entry the memory had just cleared from my mind.

Although it was very funny at the time and clearly not too serious a crime, it illustrates the degree of judgment impairment and memory loss that occurs with acute intoxication and the potential for reckless and thoughtless behavior.

Managing my drinking

I taught Kyokushin Karate and was actively involved with this physically demanding activity from 1977 to 1997, reaching the grade of 4th Dan Black belt. I got actively involved in supporting the organization in tournaments and various educational activities. Looking back, it's now difficult for me to comprehend how I managed to drink so much yet be able to compartmentalize areas of my life that were completely alcohol-free.

I organized and ran karate clubs for about twelve years and would never touch alcohol for at least a day before training, teaching or refereeing. However, after training a trip to the pub would be inevitable if time allowed. I had my special times for drinking that didn't interfere with the things in my life that required sobriety.

Years later a small group of us would take an annual cycling holiday for a few days in France. Most of us cycled every Sunday morning so it wasn't difficult from a cycling point of view as we only expected to do between 30 and 40 kilometers a day. The format was to cycle a chosen route through the beautiful French countryside whilst our luggage was transported from hotel to hotel to await our arrival. Sometimes it was organized through a travel agent where the transfers were all part of the deal and sometimes we arranged it ourselves. After a few years we stopped driving to France with the bikes on car racks as we'd done before, and started traveling by train and hiring bicycles on our arrival. Taking the train instead had the advantage that nobody needed to drive at any point and, therefore, everyone could drink from start to finish.

The drinking actually began on the train with a few bottles of wine to set things in motion as most of us routinely carried a couple in our hand luggage.

The result of long term exposure to consistently high levels of alcohol is that drunkenness occurs without the typical signs of intoxication. One's ability to function is maintained in a limited way and there is often no nausea or vomiting and the hangover effects are limited or possibly absent altogether.

I really enjoyed these trips, particularly the drinking aspect, because at that time it was very much a part of my identity. I drank heavily whenever possible and enjoyed the company of friends I had known for years. If I had my time again I might make the same decisions again. Having fun is a good thing and alcohol is often a part of that. However, I have now acknowl-edged that in my case excessive drinking extended far beyond what anyone could call normal. I recognize that the primary objective of the holiday was to drink heavily which I now see as bizarre, though at the time, it was really important to me.

These events, whether they were holidays in France, trips to London's famous Twickenham stadium for rugby matches or a day out on someone's boat, all involved alcohol. I planned my social life so that watching sport or going on holidays always created the opportunity to drink heavily.

What puzzles me is how, at that time, I really didn't consider myself to have a problem.

My concern about my drinking came much later, after I had retired from karate. Often people report that the realization gradually unfolds over period of time and that the struggle truly begins after the acknowledgement that their drinking behavior is a real problem. In the early stages it's often denied or the behavior rationalized in some way. Those who get past this will more likely succeed in resolving the problem.

I had been drinking heavily for a long time, and this behavior had become well entrenched. Late nights in the pub no longer fitted quite so well with other parts of our lives, so my drinking buddies and I organized our drinking routines to seamlessly fit in with new patterns of work and other more normal commitments. Despite the exemplary planning the alcohol consumption was still excessive and remained central to these social interactions.

Whilst I thought I had this aspect of my life well under control, it had subtly maneuvered itself into a position of prime importance to me. This was most evident if my drinking plans were disrupted in some way because I would become stressed and feel angry. It began to dawn on me that it wasn't really my free choice to drink heavily, I *needed* it. This continued until I decided that drink had become too important to me and if I allowed the pattern to roll on my life would be the worse for it.

Seeing the light

The aspect of these meet-ups that I came to dislike most was that drinking to excess became the objective in itself. It became symptomatic of a relationship with alcohol that I knew in my heart I had to change. It may not have become so much of an issue were it not for the fact that I was destroying both my body and my closest relationship.

Around this time a very good friend of mine was diagnosed with cancer of the esophagus and subsequently died of it. This particular cancer is strongly linked to excess alcohol consumption and he was a very heavy drinker. I don't know for sure if it was the alcohol that caused the cancer, but it seems likely. On reflection I think this event played a major part in my decision to change my life.

I began to take an interest in the harmful effects of alcohol consumption and after seeing it take away a good friend, I began to consider what I was doing to my own health. At that time I was taking daily medication for hypertension, gout and asthma. I became aware that my body was responding to the toxic effect of the alcohol and I developed a sense of running out of time. Looking back that seems to have been a fair assessment because these days other than an occasional use of my asthma inhaler I take no medication whatsoever.

As a practicing hypnotherapist I was used to helping people resolve issues in their lives. People often came to me for help to quit smoking, remove a phobia or lose weight, as well as a range of other issues, so I was used to working with the subconscious part of the mind to facilitate change. Through my own journey of recovery I became motivated to create an approach that would help others to remove alcohol from their lives. I felt I had something to offer and I began structuring a therapy model to achieve this.

A journey into self hypnosis

I began researching into alcohol-related issues, including its effects on health and relationships. Using that information, as well as my own understanding of how people are motivated, I began writing the script for the first Alcohol Control hypnosis CD/download.

Part of the process of creating hypnosis recordings is to listen to them. Firstly, it is with a technical objective in mind. Is the music too loud? Do all the sections of the recording come in at the right time? Is the overall pace ok?

When technical aspects of a recording are being assessed the mind is closed to any hypnotic effect because one is paying attention to the content in an analytical way and not really tuning in to the overall process. But when I'm satisfied that it is technically correct, I listen to it again as a client might. I try to relax into the process. It's important to listen to the entire recording in order to get a sense and feel for the flow throughout. By allowing myself to become immersed in the substance of the recordings I was also exposing myself to the messages and suggestions they contained. Repeated listening helped me change at the subconscious level as it would anyone else.

Many people have told me that the hypnosis recordings have helped them to make significant changes to their relationship with alcohol so it is no surprise that they had a similar effect on me.

It is quite odd really, because it's my voice I'm listening to and it's me making changes to myself but as if I were someone else.

Events and circumstances were changing how I felt about alcohol. I had lost a friend to a cancer and my marital relationship was treading water. I realized that my heavy drinking habits were largely responsible. I became very motivated to do something about my situation.

Through the hypnosis, I had changed the way I subconsciously felt about alcohol and it had occurred instantly in much the same way as when I decided I didn't want to smoke any more some years earlier. My attention at the time was focused very much on the realities of alcohol abuse and that helped encourage the necessary subconscious shift.

It's not willpower, it's not self-persuasion, nor is it aversion. It is more akin to a sea change in understanding that happens in a moment. Now, I don't have to fight alcohol or even avoid it, but my relationship with it has changed. I no longer need it. That kind of change is permanent.

After creating that first hypnosis recording I went on to develop an on-line program and created a web site to deliver it. The web program can be followed with complete anonymity and for that reason is attractive to many. Hundreds people have been through it to date.

Some of these people have made positive comments about the program so I know it makes a difference. This was another important motivation for the book.

The desire to change

So what initiates the desire to change? When you feel that motivation what can you do about it?

For me it was a combination of things, relationship issues, health concerns and the death of a friend that led to a realization of just how powerful this mind altering drug can be.

One of the most dramatic effects of alcohol is how much it changes the way you perceive yourself, others around you and the manner in which you generally interact with them. When you are in an intoxicated state your opinion of yourself and your abilities isn't necessarily that accurate.

It is true that the effects of mild to moderate drunkenness can be pleasurable for many but you do need to be wary when drinking. Caution is not so easy with a glass in your hand.

My wife rarely drinks, because she doesn't like it that much and because of the effect that drink had on her father. The fact that I drank too much often created stress and when I also behaved badly those stresses would peak, we would argue, everyone would be upset and some time would have to pass before normality resumed in the relationship.

The absence now of stressful situations, directly caused by my drinking, is one of the major benefits of my personal change. The development of problems in close personal relationships is often a motivation in seeking help. For some people, this is the issue that brings it all to a head. It could be extreme and violent arguments between partners or perhaps soft words from a confused child like "Mummy, why do you drink so much?" Typically the problem will have existed for some time before it is properly acknowledged. This contributes to the difficulty of re-establishing trust and faith in a relationship even after the alcohol issue has been addressed.

Who are you kidding?

Most people I see have made previous attempts to modify their behavior without long term success. Often people introduce strategies into their lives that don't resolve the problem but play a part in convincing them that it isn't as bad as they thought it was.

One of these is the 'abstinence delusion'. This often appears as the January 'dry' month. I know because I did it for years. I did it for one reason only, which was to convince myself that as far as alcohol was concerned I could take it or leave it. I couldn't possibly be an alcoholic because I could go without drinking for a month. I avoided alcohol in any form throughout January and the strategy had the desired effect. "I like a drink but I could stop tomorrow", I said to myself, and everyone around me. "Look! I've just gone a whole month without a drink".

This delusionary thinking kept me drinking heavily for much longer than I might have done otherwise.

Another commonly used approach is the 'keep fit' smoke-screen. Exercise is used as a psychological counter to alcohol. The belief often operating here is "If I pursue rigorous and regular exercise, I'll remain fit and strong and the alcohol can't get me". The thinking being that "only unfit, overweight and slovenly people can jeopardize their health by drinking heavily, but not me because I'm super fit". There is a belief that youth, fitness and strength are somehow an antidote to illness caused by excess alcohol consumption. Unfortunately, that's not a sensible or valid conclusion.

What is a 'Sophisticated Alcoholic'?

This is a person who does not allow alcohol to interfere with the functional part of their life. They ensure their work is not overly affected and they rarely lose control. Their drinking occurs after work, at weekends or at special events.

There are many people in this category who have already decided that they drink too much, that their relationship with alcohol has become too important to the point that it is taking over their life and that a change is needed.

It is for these people that I set out to write this book. The nature of their alcohol misuse together with their discreet and managed drinking behavior prompted its title.

Who me?

This book doesn't make any moral judgments and nor is it a treatise on all the damaging effects of excessive drinking. Your core beliefs ultimately drive your behavior and as they are held at the subconscious level they have to be changed there. This book shows you how to do that and provides tools and support so that you can do it for yourself. You can't hand responsibility to someone else to change how you feel. In the same way as getting an exercise bike or signing up for gym membership alone won't get you fit, simply buying this book won't solve your alcohol problem. You need to become personally committed to the process. You have to be involved and you have to do the work.

This book is for people who have already decided they want to drink less or not at all. It introduces a tried and tested way to do it. It explains how alcohol is used to nullify some feelings and enhance others and why people become trapped in destructive behavioral patterns.

I believe that if you truly understand why you behave this way with alcohol you will be better placed to change.

What lies beneath?

I once worked with a client that would only drink one glass of wine, two or three times a week and rarely more. He reacted badly to alcohol and always suffered the following day with a hangover but even this wasn't enough to prevent him from continuing to drink. There were other issues in his life he wasn't happy with, but because of the prominence of his alcohol problem these were just seen as unrelated and separate. He had ongoing problems with a former employer and lacked confidence about getting another job. He constantly felt tired, lacked motivation and carried around a feeling that his life was worthless.

On top of all this he always felt physically ill the day after having only a glass of wine.

By dealing with unresolved emotional issues not only did he resolve his issues with alcohol but he brought other parts of his life back on track as well.

We had met for only three or four sessions when one day he said to me that he had woken up and everything had changed. He said he felt motivated, he could see a path. The wine no longer held the importance it had held just the day before and something had shifted. He had arranged some job interviews, decided on a house move and felt like a different person.

The work we had done together addressed, as it often does,

long-standing past issues with a parent. These emotional residues were treated using Emotional Freedom Techniques – EFT, a tool introduced later in this book.

This wasn't a revelation during a therapy session but a consequence of the process. One night it all changed.

Alcohol problems are very often symptomatic of underlying emotional issues that also have an effect on other areas of our life. In other words, an alcohol problem isn't simply a problem with alcohol. Drinking excessively is usually a symptom of something else and hardly ever the root problem itself.

It is not atypical for drinkers to harbor other issues. Excessive and uncontrolled drinking is often just the one that has risen to the top of the pile.

Knowing and understanding this suggests that the addiction is often not the 'real' problem but due to its inherent self-perpetuating nature it certainly warrants some attention in its own right. It isn't alcohol alone that makes you an alcoholic. It's not solely the chemical component of alcohol that makes it addictive to the biochemistry of the body and creates a physical dependence. It also can't all be explained by your genes. Most importantly, it's not irreversible or unchangeable. It's a habit and one that is often being used to compensate for other situations. For the most part, it's an acquired behavior that you are able to change and I'm going to show you how you can do that.

The destruction already savaged on a life through excessive consumption may affect the processes needed to bring things back on track but it doesn't alter the fact that it's not fixed, it's not inexorable. It is possible for everyone to make changes to their relationship with alcohol. The way you set about it might vary but the principles behind making a permanent change remain the same.

Renewed hope
The book is also for 'recovering alcoholics'. There is a world of

difference in fighting the temptation of alcohol, of being afraid to ever allow a sip to pass your lips and becoming truly ambivalent towards it so that you are in a position that you could 'take it or leave it'. The recovering alcoholic has already done the hardest work because they have brought their life back on track. However, the problem still exists and they know better than anyone else that without clearing it, their life can only be saved by total abstinence. Some people, however, will eventually want more than to reside in this 'no-man's land'; some of those 'in recovery' may want to free themselves, once and for all, from the fear of relapse that stalks them every day of their lives

Three steps to change

The book is divided into three sections.

The first is dedicated to understanding the causes of alcohol addiction. We will see how the medical world currently conceptualizes and classifies alcohol-related problems and the shortfalls of using this model. This understanding is fundamental to demonstrating why the model presented in this book is necessary and how it varies from current practice. I will then introduce concepts you may not have considered before and offer renewed hope to drinkers who continue to struggle but can't see another way forward.

The second section introduces you to the tools you will need to help facilitate real change. I will show you how to deal with the underlying causes of your drinking problem. It explains how hypnosis can make dramatic changes to the way you feel and explains why that is.

I will also introduce a truly amazing approach called Emotional Freedom Techniques (EFT) and explain how it can be used to process long-standing emotional distress and alter dysfunctional beliefs that underlie the need to drink to excess. I'll show you how you can also use EFT to overcome subconscious resistance to making a permanent change to your relationship with alcohol.

The third section proposes a practical, step-by-step program for you to follow, integrating the techniques you have learnt to bring about real and lasting change.

Of course, the tools and techniques described in this book do not represent the only way to achieve change or to alter core beliefs. There are other mechanisms and therapies, including many mainstream ones that can also help. See this book as adding a layer of sophistication to the understanding and management of this complex, multifaceted problem. If, from reading this you gain an increased sense of control and a sense that change is truly achievable it will have been a very worthwhile venture indeed.

I want to re-emphasize one important point that makes this approach different from the rest. The conventional or accepted approach to alcoholism is to provide support and assistance to help sufferers resist the urge to drink. It also highlights, often subtly using clever forms of communication, the downsides of the destructive behavior. Addicts establish a delicate balance between the desire to drink and the consequences of satiating that desire. This approach is quite rational and in some cases effective but quite different from removing the fundamental reasons driving and maintaining the problem. The conventional model comes to the problem from the opposite direction with a focus on suppression rather than removal of the underlying cause. However, having said that, it is true that for some this may be the only approach that they have encountered that 'works' for them. When the cycle of despair is so extreme, it is sometimes necessary to put a stick in the spokes of the wheel to stop it in its tracks immediately. For this reason, I applaud the work that support organizations, such as Alcoholics Anonymous, do to help desperate people toward 'recovery'. But I'll also explain why such an approach can only be a lifelong management strategy and why it cannot truly eliminate those potent desires.

Changing behavior

I consider alcoholism to be, in the vast majority of cases, a reactive behavior and not an incurable illness. Behavior can change.

Things that help facilitate behavioral change:

- Information about the effects of alcohol (including health risks)
- Understanding the dynamics of the problem
- Enlightenment and a renewed motivation to change
- Resolution of the unresolved emotional issues that underpin, drive or maintain the behavior
- Challenging and correcting the dysfunctional core beliefs that validate the behavior

Summary

I have completely changed my relationship with alcohol and so can you. This book will help you achieve this goal with its practical approach and the introduction of effective tools and techniques to support the process.

Excessive drinking is far more widespread, amongst otherwise balanced and upstanding people, than is generally thought. The very nature of this controlled excess, carefully integrated into a busy lifestyle, ensures that it doesn't make headlines. Many people, including those with professional and responsible careers manage an excessive alcohol habit in exactly this way and this is one factor that contributes to it assuming a sense of normality and a degree of invisibility.

This book is for those *'sophisticated alcoholics'* who have decided they are ready for change

Chapter 2

A Psychiatrist's perspective
(Dr James Kustow)

Setting the scene

In England, approximately 90% of adults drink alcohol. This equates to about 40 million people. The majority do not experience problems and enjoy its pleasurable effects responsibly as a social pastime. However, it is estimated that about a quarter of the adult population drink in a way that is potentially or actually harmful to them.

Alcohol is a psychoactive substance which is rapidly absorbed in the gut. It is then transferred in the blood to the brain where it has an immediate effect on a number of brain functions including coordination, judgment and mood. Over the longer term it increases the risk of both mental health problems (depression, anxiety, other addictions, self harm and suicide) and physical health problems. Almost every organ in the body is vulnerable to its toxic effects and it is thought to be a risk factor for over 60 different diseases, including heart disease, strokes, high blood pressure, liver cirrhosis and various different cancers. Alcohol does more harm to more people than all the illegal drugs grouped together.

There are different categories of alcohol misuse on a spectrum between 'hazardous' drinkers through to those who are 'severely dependant', with individuals moving backwards and forwards between categories at different points during their lives. Understandably, due to limited resources, attention is primarily focused on the severe end of the spectrum as it is these people who create the most social problems (offending behavior, homelessness etc) and cost the country most in terms of medical care.

There are limited government-run services available to those whose problem remains to some extent contained or self-managed, especially when it is having only an insidious, long term effect on health. This large cohort of people have specific, and arguably more complex needs and it is for them, principally, that this book has been tailored.

Conceptualizing and classifying

There has always been confusion with respect to terminology around alcohol problems. On the most basic level, how you differentiate between 'use' and 'misuse'. We talk about being 'dependent' on alcohol - what does being this actually mean? For many the most important question of all is what makes someone an 'alcoholic'?

Alcohol dependence is a syndrome (collection of symptoms) that, if present, indicates someone has more serious and long standing problems and more complex needs. It tends to be on a spectrum of severity with the more severe end of the spectrum experiencing significant *alcohol withdrawal* symptoms with abrupt abstinence. They may be maintaining the drinking habit to avoid the withdrawal symptoms. Consequently, dependent individuals may drink heavily on a daily basis over prolonged periods. These people will generally require medically-assisted alcohol withdrawal or 'detoxification'. Government figures suggest that 4% of adults in England are alcohol-dependent and this is likely to be a significant underestimation. If you fall into this category and think you require a detoxification, it is essential to speak openly with your GP or local alcohol service for advice and support.

The notion of alcoholism as a disease is centered on whether or not there is evidence of alcohol dependence. Consequently, the 'Alcohol Dependence Syndrome', a term coined by Edwards and Gross in 1976, has informed the main psychiatric diagnostic classification systems since.

Alcohol use disorders are classified along with other psychiatric disorders in both of the two main diagnostic systems used today throughout the world:

- DSM IV (Diagnostic and Statistical Manual of mental disorders) is the US based system
- ICD IO (International Statistical Classification of Diseases) is the European equivalent, created by the World Health Organization

(See Appendix 1a for further detail on Definitions and Classification)

Both systems, which are very similar to each other, use a categorical, rule-based approach to diagnosis. They have lists of criteria that, if met, qualify for different diagnoses. Both have evolved over the last half century or so with at least four separate updates, the most recent being in the early 1990s.

The 'Disease model' of alcohol is not new and throughout history has attracted controversy. The model implies that there is a clear delineation between 'alcoholics' (or problem drinkers) and other healthy individuals. It suggests that a diagnosis should be made, a cause (biological or psychological) sought and the appropriate management plan put in place, in much the same way that it is with other chronic medical 'conditions'.

This widely accepted model can be seen as taking the onus of the responsibility away from the individual, in doing so reducing unhelpful shame, however, it may also function to remove a person's sense of control and agency. It is the model that is promoted by Alcoholics Anonymous and it adheres to the concept 'once an addict, always an addict'.

If any aspect of alcoholism should be seen as a physical 'illness' it is alcohol dependence. After all, it has a recognizable set of clear-cut physiological features and it responds well to medical intervention. In simple terms, you either have it or you don't! It is important to remember, however, that this distinction is primarily for diagnostic and statistical purposes and the reality is a little less clear cut.

The terms *'alcoholic'* and *'alcoholism'* have been loosely applied, yet often said with an air of certainty, for over 150 years. Magnus Hoss in Sweden first coined the term 'alcoholic' to describe people who suffered *negative consequences of alcohol use.* However, interestingly, none of the criteria in the current diagnostic formulations use the terms. In fact, as a whole, the scientific community has struggled to unite for the last two centuries in defining and classifying alcohol use disorders.

Perhaps the time has come to challenge existing paradigms and take back the control. If alcoholism is a disease, maybe we should try to shift the focus from simply managing it to finding effective ways of eliminating it completely.

Causation

Over the last couple of hundred years a variety of 'scientific' models concerned with the cause of alcoholism have emerged. They have been heavily influenced by the more general intellectual perspectives of human behavior prevalent at the respective times and in many cases they have competed with each other for centre stage.

Biology has often taken a predominant role, more latterly driving the pharmacological agenda which is set the challenge of artificially correcting the altered biology. Psychological factors have gained prominence at various times particularly with the advent of the psychoanalytic movement that focused attention on early life experience. In other periods, social and cultural factors have been considered the chief culprits. The reality, however, is that all three domains – biological, psychological and socio-cultural all play a part and need to be considered when discussing etiology or cause.

The 'Bio-Psycho-Social' model of alcoholism has been cited

now for a number of years as a 'capture all' for this and other similarly complex syndromes or illness processes. Much debate exists as to the relative importance of individual factors and at which points in the causative pathway they exert their influence.

Family history

Alcohol problems clearly run in families. Children of parents with alcohol dependence are four times more likely to develop the same problem. Research has also demonstrated that children removed from alcoholic families and placed in non-alcoholic ones have still shown problems, demonstrating a possible genetic association. However, the familial nature of the disorder clearly cannot be explained by genes alone. Whilst there is clearly some genetic involvement, its significance seems to be smaller or less clear-cut than once thought.

The role of nurture and learnt behavior is fundamentally important. In particular, how these 'environmental' factors interact with the genetic ones. We learn by observing others and we tend to imitate our parents and other influential figures. In addition, having an alcoholic parent can and does result in significant emotional disturbance, something that in itself predisposes to the misuse of alcohol.

Family related risk factors for alcohol problems include poor attachment, the absence of love and support, excessive parental punishment or laxity, unhealthy communication styles and high levels of conflict in the home. Traumatic experience that occurs may remain unintegrated leaving residual, unresolved emotional distress. This distress feeds the alcohol problem, essentially driving it.

Brain chemistry

There is some evidence to support that dopamine dysregulation is involved in alcoholism. Dopamine is a brain hormone (neurotransmitter) that is important in mood, reward and general well being. Molecules of the neurotransmitter attach to dopamine receptors in the synaptic clefts (gaps) between neurons (brain cells). One variant of the dopamine receptor, D2, results in reduced function in the dopamine system (resulting in low dopamine levels) and has been shown in some populations to predispose to alcohol dependence. The D3 receptor is also thought to play an important role.

The reason for the association is that alcohol increases dopamine, which is the brain chemical directly responsible for its pleasurable effects. This artificial increase in dopamine levels compensates for (or some would argue 'self-medicates') the lowered baseline state. However, alcohol itself, used excessively, can disrupt the dopamine balance in the brain so cause and effect always needs to be considered.

Low levels of dopamine in the frontal lobe of the brain are also thought to be partly responsible for the symptoms of *Attention Deficit Hyperactivity Disorder (ADHD)*. Amongst others, these include poor impulse control and increased sensation seeking behavior, both of which are clear precursors of addictive behavior. Addiction problems, including to alcohol, are massively over represented in individuals with ADHD. The condition was previously thought only to affect children, however, clear evidence now exists that it continues into adulthood in a large percentage of cases. The prevalence of adult ADHD may be as high as 3-4% of the population meaning that this only recently understood disorder may play a highly important role in the debate on alcoholism and addiction in general, particularly given the fact that it can be effectively treated with medication.

There are other neurotransmitter systems involved in mediating the effects of alcohol. The GABA and Glutamate system have been shown to be particularly important. The GABA network is the brain's primary inhibitory system and the Glutamate one, excitatory. The sedating nature of alcohol is due to the fact that it increases GABA function and decreases Glutamate function. Genetic variants of the receptors for these neurotransmitters are thought to, in part; determine one's sensitivity to alcohol.

A deficiency in levels of Serotonin, a neurotransmitter important in the stability of mood, is associated with a vulnerability to alcoholism. Serotonin is also thought to underlie cravings for alcohol.

Even when there are clear physiological disturbances, it is important to understand that the brain (and the mind) can exercise a significant degree of control over the physiology, evidenced no more clearly than with the potent 'Placebo effect'. It is the individual's ability to influence and alter their physiology that is one of the key messages of this book.

Alcohol as a cause

It is critical to understand that the overuse of alcohol itself can be considered as a cause of at least some aspects of the problem. In the same way as smoking increases the risk of lung cancer, continual abuse of alcohol is likely to lead to alcoholism. Those individuals who are predisposed are more susceptible.

Regular and excessive alcohol use effects changes both in the brain and the rest of the body which themselves serve to drive the ongoing heavy use, spiraling the problem out of control. Drinking no longer becomes a choice. Thinking patterns distort and over time the personality changes. To complicate matters, alcohol is often used to manage the additional stress of the psychological addiction and soon enough tolerance and dependence develop taking the problem into more physiological realms.

The key question is how to break this cycle effectively. Is it possible to undo these changes? The answer lies not only in managing the disturbed biology, by allow the system to rebalance through abstinence, but also by addressing psychological factors including unresolved traumatic memory and unhelpful and limiting beliefs.

Psychological models of alcoholism

Differentiating biological from psychological is in fact a complex task as it becomes clear that the two are very much interwoven and have bi-directional effects. It is the effect of the psychology on the biology that is of primary interest in this book and that will be explored in much more detail later.

I will therefore give only a superficial overview of this topic. There are a handful of psychological theories or models that purport to explain either why alcoholism occurs in the first place or why it is maintained. In reality, they all tell a part of the story.

The story really begins with the Psychodynamic movement which focused its attention on early attachment issues, a 'fixation at the oral stage' and the self-destructive nature of addictions in general.

Behavioral models include Classical and Operant conditioning. Classical conditioning goes some way to provide an understanding of cravings and subsequent relapse by showing how, as a result of repeated associations, people develop an enhanced response to alcohol-related cues. Operant Conditioning (or learning) teaches us how the pleasurable effects of alcohol are particularly good at countering stress, at least in the short-term, and how this 'learnt' association gets reinforced over time resulting in the routine use of alcohol to cope with stressful situations or even its continual use to attempt to avoid the stress in the first place.

Social Learning Theory shows us how human learning is acquired via observation and imitation. Adolescents tend to model their own drinking behavior on that of their parents, other family members or other people that they look up to (including celebrities and peers).

Then a shift came, moving from more behavioral-based

models to an increased emphasis on the role of cognitions (or one's thinking). The belief system attracted a lot of interest, in particular the area of 'expectancies' (beliefs held about what outcomes are expected from a behavior). It was demonstrated that people who believe they have consumed alcohol typically act in line with that belief, even if they have not. In demonstrating the power of beliefs, this work gave an important focus for intervention which has become the central tenant of cognitive therapy (or Cognitive Behavioral Therapy as a whole). 'Self efficacy' or put more simply, confidence, around one's ability to control urges to drink have also been extensively explored. Individuals lacking in confidence in their ability to manage their drinking tend to develop more serious problems with alcohol. Again beliefs show their potent influence.

Understanding how thought processes, beliefs and a sense of self efficacy influences perception around drinking (or more importantly, stopping or cutting down) is central to this book's ethos. What sets this book apart, however, is the fact that it is introducing new and effective tools and techniques to facilitate real psychological change at the body (or subconscious) level rather than through rational, conscious logic alone.

Socio-cultural influences

Widening the focus slightly, there are a number of socio-cultural influences that need to be considered in the debate on causation. We have already touched on the role of the family and the powerful effect of 'modeling'. The quality of the interaction between family members (especially with parents) and the home environment in general is of prime importance as is the acknowledgement and awareness of the protective effects of a healthy, happy family environment. Peer relationships have been shown to be fundamentally important, with a drinking culture amongst one's social group being an extremely powerful predictor of alcohol use. This is both due to the pressure to conform and the fact that adolescents tend to seek out friends whose behaviors, values and attitudes mirror their own.

A study conducted in the UK in the early 1970's looked at the occupations of individuals dying from alcoholic liver disease (cirrhosis). It found that pub owners, bar workers and sailors were at a much higher risk than the general population (up to 16 times in the case of pub owners). It suggested that availability, cost and exposure (i.e. working in the manufacture, distribution or sale of alcohol) were factors that significantly influenced consumption.

Some of the cultural beliefs around drinking will be explored further in the book and their influence should not be underestimated, nor should the role that the alcohol industry plays in the story. Its power is no more intensely felt than through the medium of advertising, which is constantly growing in sophistication. Often subtle messages portraying alcohol as fun, confidence-building and sexy are everywhere and they are constantly being integrated at a subconscious level.

Finally, there needs to be some acknowledgement of the impact of government policy as it is well established that the availability of alcohol is a major factor in determining how much is consumed by a country. The government has the power to influence availability through pricing and via licensing laws. Taxing alcohol raises its price and is used, in addition to generating significant revenue for the treasury, to help limit misuse.

Conventional treatment overview

The approach to the management of alcohol problems can be viewed from a societal perspective, facilitated through public health initiatives or related directly to the individual, with whom this book is primarily concerned. Individuals require an individualized approach that takes into consideration their level of motivation to change, the degree of severity of the problem, the wider context and their life experience. The approach should without doubt be guided by the latest evidence but it is also important for it not to be too rigid and closed minded in it appraisal.

An essential component of management is effective recognition and good quality, person-centered assessment. Exploring potential causes and risk factors together with the person, taking a non-judgmental stance, helps create rapport and trust and can relieve feelings of blame or shame. Understanding the individual and their specific needs, vulnerabilities and environment is crucial and this takes time. Good communication skills are of utmost importance especially if time is limited. Confidentiality protocols must be rigorous.

Currently within the NHS, the treatment of alcohol problems tends to be focused on the more severe end of the spectrum and could be accused of neglecting those with less visible difficulties and those who are early on in their journey. Due to limited resources, there often exists a 'firefighting' mentality and interventions, especially on first contact, tend to be slightly crude, focused disproportionately on risk and usually very generic and standardized (in order to collect good data for audit). All too often, the therapeutic focus lies with establishing the person's motivation to change and subsequently the logistics of arranging a detoxification. There tends to be an over reliance on pharmacological interventions which, without question, can be helpful but are only a part of the story. In my experience, there is often not enough focus on the relationship with the client, the preparation phase, the *process* of stopping and the planning of aftercare and ongoing support.

Those with less severe alcohol problems tend to turn to 3rd sector voluntary organizations or private sector clinics where the quality of assessment and intervention varies considerably. There is a heavy weighting towards the 12-step (Alcohol Anonymous) model which is popular with those for whom it has given a lifeline. However, such an approach still attracts significant controversy for its religious overtones and the criticism that it fosters hopelessness and over-identification with the disease model.

AA, as it is popularly known, was founded in 1935 in Ohio and the 12 steps (or 'traditions') were introduced in 1946. 'Addicts' are encouraged to attend regular meetings which have a set structure and allow a space for people to tell their story and access support from others. There is an emphasis on anonymity, altruism and powerlessness. There is a process of mentorship, with new recruits being encouraged to identify a 'sponsor', someone who is an experienced fellow alcoholic, to help support them through the structured 12 step program.

Psychological approaches are available in the NHS and are offered or integrated but, on the whole, tend to be time limited and often slightly narrow in their scope. The psychological approaches, included and appraised in the new draft NICE guidelines of alcohol (2010), are listed in *Appendix 1b*. Probably the most widely used therapeutic approaches, other than the Alcoholics Anonymous 12-step program and general psychoeducation, are Motivational Enhancement Therapy (MET) and Cognitive Behavioral Therapy (CBT). Both are very practical and focused in the present *(See Appendix 1c for an overview of these approaches)*.

With the progressive decline in the availability of psychodynamic therapy, in favor of more 'here and now', practical approaches such as CBT, paired with a delay in the mainstream taking on board some of the newer body-orientated therapeutic approaches available, due in part to the limited available evidence, the critical work at the subconscious and body level is often being neglected.

Summary and future developments

Alcohol can be used and enjoyed sensibly but for some individuals, in certain situations and for a variety of reasons, it can achieve disproportionate salience, resulting in progressive neglect of other interests, a deterioration of health and a state of dependence and addiction. The resultant behavioral characteristics and thinking distortions are shared with other drugs of abuse and other forms of (non-substance) addiction.

When discussing etiology or cause a useful framework is to consider *biological, psychological* and *socio-cultural* factors that may be exerting an influence. Additionally, in conceptualizing addictions in general, it is important to take into account the *user*, the *substance* (and its effects on the body) and the *circumstances*.

Regarding treatment, in my personal view, there is a slightly unhelpful over alliance to the 'disease model', an over reliance on pharmacological interventions and a relative neglect of the underlying emotional distress, unresolved past traumas and limiting beliefs that invariably play an important role.

I believe that it is necessary for people to feel different about alcohol at a 'gut' level rather than simply developing a rational understanding of the problem and overlaying behavioral restrictions and limitations that usually invoke resistance and, at the very least, absorb unhealthy amounts of energy to sustain longer term. If changes are not made at a deeper level, relapse is always 'just around the corner' and with each 'slip up' the sense of hopelessness and desperation is reinforced.

We cannot completely disregard the role that our physiology plays. There is little doubt that as a result of certain personality traits some people are more vulnerable to addiction. The key question is however, how much can emotions and beliefs alter physiology and shape personality? Will the physiology normalize if the emotions are processed and beliefs addressed? And could it be that the personality changes observed are actually secondary to the alcohol problem?

What is very clear to me is that if we were able to identify the unresolved emotional issues and unprocessed traumas from the past and then process them effectively, we would have moved a few steps closer in the ultimate quest to find something closer to a 'cure' for this devastating condition.

This book will open your mind and introduce you to some powerful self-help techniques whilst guiding you through a rewarding process of change. I hope you enjoy it.

Chapter 3

Exploring alcoholism

As we have seen in the previous chapter, defining this condition is not easy. It often depends upon who needs the definition and what purpose it serves. From that perspective it's helpful to create one that works for you. Perhaps the most useful definition is one that helps to answer the question, 'do I have a problem with alcohol?' In my view the following are useful indicators that there may be a problem. I hope they help.

- *You cannot stop for a sustained period*
- *Your drinking has become compulsive or destructive in some way*
- *Your drinking exceeds levels you know to be generally acceptable*
- *Your drinking exceeds levels acceptable to those close to you*

Let's get the label out of the way

If you can relate to some of the criteria discussed in the previous chapter, you may well have a problem with alcohol. If the term 'alcoholic' makes you feel uncomfortable and you would rather describe yourself in some other way that is less severe, like 'heavy drinker', then do that because the name doesn't really matter. If you believe you are physically (physiologically) dependent on alcohol, I would advise you to seek medical advice and manage the withdrawal syndrome safely. Regardless of where you lie on the spectrum, it is important that you acknowledge that you place too much value on alcohol and have difficulty in controlling your behavior in this area. So the real question might be, "how do I begin to deal with such a problem?"

Challenging the entrenched disease model

We have established that there is no single accepted cause of alcoholism. It is considered multifactoral. Little attention is paid to unresolved emotional problems as most of the focus lies on the behavior itself which is seen as a problem in its own right. Equally, there is no accepted cure for the problem, with the prevailing view regarding treatment, best illustrated by the AA model, being to simply 'manage' it indefinitely. This usually means complete abstinence with ongoing supervision and support.

Whilst this is certainly helpful for some people it doesn't aim for resolution, rather containment. Importantly, our objective is to completely eliminate the problem rather than suppress it. However, for some people enforced abstinence through a support network might well be a necessary first step.

Alcohol misuse is a behavior and, in my view, it's unhelpful to refer to it as an illness except in the sense that it often causes serious illness. Society needs to find better ways to deal with this ever increasing problem. I feel we need to look at addictive behavior in a slightly different light because conventional approaches don't work well enough or often enough for us to be satisfied. Additionally, such methods still present an uncertain and often bleak future even for those who initially found them useful.

The mainstream approach to alcohol addiction and other similarly destructive addictions is rather akin to continually topping up your car radiator when there is a water leak. It's inconvenient and time consuming but it works for a while. As long as you keep topping up you can continue to drive, but there is an ever present risk of complete breakdown if the leak gets bigger or the top up water supply runs out.

In an emergency, of course, topping up is essential to keep going until you can get to a garage where the leak can be identified and properly repaired.

There are real problems with such an approach in the case of alcoholism. It is difficult to do and the energy used to suppress the desire can stress the system. Additionally it supports and propagates a belief that the problem is entrenched and that there is no alternative. Viewing alcoholism as a disease which is caused by drink itself is counter intuitive, defeatist and overly simplistic.

If alcoholism, alcohol dependency, heavy drinking, binge drinking or any other name you care to use is an illness for which the outlook is only ever going to be grim where is the incentive to recover? If it is so firmly encoded in your genes, then how can you possibly hope to win the battle?

No wonder then that it is considered to be incurable, with abstinence and long term, ongoing support purported to be the only way for people to rejoin a meaningful and constructive life. What a depressing scenario!

The ethos of this defeatist thinking is captured in the Alcoholics Anonymous (AA) 12 step program which is widely considered to be the gold standard approach to the problem. It has been shown to 'work' in studies, though with significant levels of relapse. Perhaps it is not the only way. Such wide acceptance almost certainly limits the search to find a better approach.

See *(Appendix 5)* for both the original 12 step program and a more modern form. There are variations on the twelve step process employed by a number of other institutions and, with few exceptions, they share similar fundamental flaws. People who have experienced the AA method often report that it seeks to replace one obsession with another, the AA process itself. I don't say this as a negative criticism of the organization because their objectives are laudable and honest and they undoubtedly seek to promote recovery. However, having a strong brand and philosophy and promoting the approach as the only way, doesn't mean that it necessarily is.

Moreover, I don't see permanent abstinence as necessary and I explain in detail the potential pitfalls of seeing things in such black and white terms.

Scratching below the surface

Alcohol often starts as being the 'treatment' to pre-existing problems before it becomes a problem in itself.

People drink for a reason and this approach clearly works to a degree or they simply wouldn't do it. The desire to drink is a feeling, a low grade anxiety which, at times, becomes strong enough to be considered a craving so powerful that it can take precedence over all other things until it is fulfilled.

What kind of emotions might be driving this need to self medicate? Can they be identified? Can they be traced back to a source or an event? Might there also be secondary emotions that are helping to maintain the problem?

If it were possible to limit or eliminate the underlying negative emotions, would that modify the addictive and compulsive behavior and if it did would that prevent these feelings from resurfacing? It seems quite bizarre to me that we as a society favor the suppression of feelings as the way to go rather than aiming to remove them altogether.

If you ask a heavy drinker why they do it you are likely to get the response "because I like it", but for those who would respond this way it is worth considering that one's likes and dislikes are simply just a function of perception and belief. If you believe you like/dislike something then you will retain that position until something happens to change your view.

Whatever the underlying reasons are for drinking to excess it's clear that alcohol resolves, satisfies or anaesthetizes them, albeit temporarily. This book is only concerned with excessive or dysfunctional drinking and not balanced or 'normal' drinking behavior. After all drinking is firmly entrenched in our culture; it is a part of how we live our lives. It is entirely possible to enjoy it responsibly without concern just as we might do with exercise, food, sex or even coffee.

An acquired taste?

Consider the situation of two people sitting at a table about to eat anchovies. One person likes anchovies and the other doesn't, but both of them have agreed to eat some. This isn't a problem for the person who likes them but is clearly a challenge for the person who doesn't.

The substance of the anchovy is identical for both parties. When the scent of the fish is first registered at the level of the nose, the effect on the smell receptors is the same. As the first touch is felt on the tongue or the lips, the chemical signals generated are the same for both parties because the point where 'taste' is determined has not yet been reached.

The decision as to whether this is a 'good' or a 'bad' thing, whether it is liked or disliked, happens after those signals have been received by the brain. The complex process of perception can be conceptualized as interplay between different brain regions which integrates past experience and results in the evaluation of those chemical and electrical signals. Whether or not we express pleasure or disgust will be influenced by a preconception of what kind of experience it will be, whether that is derived by direct past experience or acquired by a more indirect mechanism. A child, for example, who has never tasted a Brussel Sprout, may express a dislike of them using a set of perceptions formed from other related experience e.g. an established dislike of a similar shape, color or texture.

The key point is that even though the initial physical stimulus and the signals produced are the same for both people, one person expresses pleasure and the other feels revulsion simply due to differences in their perceptual processes. The brain has already made the like/don't like decision and this appraisal is reinforced each time the stimulus is encountered.

Oddly enough, strong drink is always unpleasant the first time it is tried. Imagine the response of a ten-year-old child who is given a taste of whisky. It takes many years of cultural conditioning to develop the perception that drinking alcohol is a pleasant experience. A large part of this conditioning effect is the relentless social promotion and advertising that alcohol attracts. One learns to like alcohol because the emotional need to comply at some point outweighs the unpleasantness of the experience.

Likes and dislikes are usually learned behaviors and are not purely inherent genetic or cellular functions, so drinking because you "like it" is an irrelevant concept. If you can learn to like it, the reverse must also be true – you can learn to dislike alcohol.

How much is too much?

Used in modest quantities, the 'loosening up' effect is often one of the benefits people report. It is still satisfying a need but at these levels it is not considered to be physically or socially harmful to us. We all have our likes and dislikes and ideally we want to pursue the things we like without feeling compelled to indulge past the point of physical harm. There is no reason why this cannot be the case with alcohol.

As a society we employ concepts of what is normal and what is excessive drinking behavior. How do we decide this and what do we consider to be normal?

From the perspective of personal change, it is always the individual who has to make this decision, ideally together with those close to them. As we have heard, there are established and very visible public health guidelines on safe drinking with formal, medically-based recommendations for maximum daily or weekly intake which may provide some guidance *(see Appendix 1 for further detail)*.

Drink-related criminal offences, including motoring convictions are external factors that may also highlight a problem and indicate that someone is drinking to excess. Similarly, out of character, violent or dangerous behavior, frequent work absences or unexplained physical illness may also suggest a problem. Such a realization will present at different times for different people and will depend enormously on their individual lifestyles and levels of function. There will usually be a range of indicators that highlight the presence of a problem.

Perhaps it's true that were it not for the medical risks associated with excess alcohol consumption the majority of 'sophisticated alcoholics' may not consider their drinking to be a problem. It is likely, for example that amongst this cohort, overtly antisocial behavior is less of an issue. Rather than displaying riotous behavior when intoxicated, the more mature and organized drinker will settle for no more than some animated discussion followed by sleep. Charging down the high street or throwing up in taxis isn't the style of this book's target audience. It may well be that over indulgence might not be considered so dangerous were it not for the major health issues caused by excessive alcohol consumption,

The reality is, however, that drinking catches up with you. Heavy drinking is highly likely to cause an illness of some description at some time. Often the resultant health problem experienced by an individual isn't automatically associated with drinking by them at all. The time span between the cause and effect is often many years. For example the 70 year old with digestion problems may not link that condition with their many years of consumption even though it is a well established cause of such compromised health.

"I could do with a drink"

Whether it is for celebration or commiseration, a quiet evening in or some other occasion, a need is being attended to when you have a drink. Why does alcohol work when you are happy, when you have had some great news or when it's your birthday? How can it also work when you have lost your job, your wife has left or a loved one has died? Why do you feel the need to keep up with the group on a boys'/girls' night out?

Happiness, sadness or a need to belong are all feelings that, initially at least, can be suppressed, enhanced or maintained by alcohol. At least, the mind believes this to be true, because if it weren't then the drinking behavior would cease. It is also evident that whatever the reasons are to drink, they feel stronger and more powerful than the opposing physical, mental and material destruction that results. Knowing that drinking is slowly destroying your life yet being unable to control your behavior is testament to the potency of these underlying emotional needs.

The question that needs to be asked is "What drives these feelings"? Are they mental, emotional, genetic or environmental and do we have any control over it? These issues were explored in the last chapter in detail and in the next chapter I will draw the focus in to the powerful role of belief.

It is important to acknowledge and understand that there are rational reasons that cause people to become dependent upon substances that are damaging to them. Alcohol is often the substance of choice because it is legal, readily available, cheap and ruthlessly promoted, often in subtle ways such as sponsorship and placement as well as overt advertising. In the short term alcohol works effectively to modify emotions. When these uncomfortable emotions are felt again, instinctively, the same solution is applied. This pattern continues to be reinforced to the point that physical damage and serious life problems result. Unresolved and long standing emotional issues therefore drive the drinking behavior, as under the influence, they are temporarily abated.

Would you pay for a television that didn't work or maintain roadside assistance if they never came out to help when you needed them? Would you continue to buy fruit from a market stall if it was always past its best and rotten by the time you wanted to eat it? Importantly, for most people the answer to all of these questions is a resounding no. In just the same way that you wouldn't do any of the above, you also wouldn't continue to drink excessively if it didn't work for you, if it didn't satisfy an important need.

Neither you nor I would use alcohol if it didn't serve a function for us in the moment. It satisfies specific needs. These are explored in Module 2 of the program in more detail with suggestions for dealing with this issue. Part of the problem surrounding alcohol is that in the short term it can seem like an effective solution.

In a sense alcohol presents itself as a 'cure' and not a problem but it is the long term damage caused by this particular form of self medication that makes it a poor choice of intervention for dealing with negative emotions.

Chapter 4

The role of psychology

Important psychological themes
underlying drinking behavior

Meeting social expectations

We all have a vision of ourselves that we strive to maintain and present to the outside world. The things that affect that vision include cultural and social norms and expectations. There is a powerful incentive to maintain the projected image of ourselves unless there is a very good reason not to.

In our modern day culture, the promotion and use of alcohol strongly supports a number of characteristics that we perceive to be desirable for both men and women, even though the specific situations may sometimes vary.

For men, the use of alcohol (sometimes to excess) is seen as manly with all that embodies. It is used to impress whilst engendering a sense of belonging to the elite of manhood. For a woman it can promote a heightened sense of femininity and sexiness, suggest intimacy, rebellion or equality.

There is a traditional view that sees women as being 'weaker' than men and there are many social and cultural factors that are supportive of it. Inequality in pay and lack of opportunity in the workplace represent some of them. A kind of leveling through behavior can be seen as addressing some of these issues, after all to cement such 'equality' why not behave like men in some way? Adopting similarly excessive drinking patterns is one way of achieving this. Equality, enhancement and superiority of the female is a concept ruthlessly exploited in alcohol advertising.

Once the relationship between drinking and those desirable

characteristics within ourselves that we publish to the outside world is established, there is then a psychological need to maintain the behavior. To alter behavior without a good and accepted reason creates stress, doubt and insecurity, particularly in group and social interactions.

If you do not behave as expected it confuses the subconscious until some justification is presented that is understood and accepted to explain the changes. This stress makes us feel bad and for the most part we want to avoid it, so wherever there is this expectation that we will drink alcohol in a particular manner we tend to adhere. It's difficult to behave differently without creating emotional stress unless a fundamental change is made to our core beliefs. Emotionally we will constantly try to comply with whatever promises we might have made to ourselves beforehand. It is common to be determined not to drink, or to drink less, before partial inebriation sets in. However, people who are logically and rationally in charge of their actions often break their resolve not to drink too much. Part of the reason is the altered mental state that alcohol induces and another part is the unremitting subconscious imperative to maintain our identity. These pressures easily override any casual intention we may have displayed beforehand. Alcohol reduces our capacity for rational judgment and alters the way we process information to the detriment of sound reasoning. It does this because it is a mind altering drug, and in combination with the need to meet social expectations it presents a powerful opponent. There are circumstances, however, that allow this behavioral change to be temporarily accepted by others with no damage to reputation and little disapproval, absolving the person of the need to meet normal expectations. Being pregnant, driving (perhaps having drawn the short straw and so having to drive) or being on medication that disagrees with alcohol are generally accepted as valid excuses to abstain. 'I'm not well' is another, and a particularly bizarre version of this is when you have alcohol poisoning caused by excess consumption the previous day. Ironically enough this is regarded as a perfectly acceptable reason for not drinking whilst actually heightening the expectation to drink heavily in future. Most importantly it does not question the wisdom of the rest of the group continuing to drink heavily. Simply put, if you have a reputation of drinking others under the table then you will do everything you can to sustain it.

Belonging to the group

We need to be liked and we need to belong. Activities that support those needs make us feel good and those that don't make us feel bad. For the most part we display a natural tendency to do things that make us feel good. The need to belong is powerful and is one of the main influences in who we become and the view we have of the world.

By way of example, I have never met anyone who started smoking because they liked it. The usual effect of the first cigarette is coughing followed in some cases by retching and vomiting. Yet this rather grim induction is often completed despite the adverse physical reactions. You might wonder what need was so great as to demand such endurance. What might be so rewarding at the end of this initiation so as to motivate someone to persevere to the point that the activity becomes easier to endure and then becomes so compulsive that they find it really difficult to stop?

The desire to be acknowledged as part of a group is strong, particularly when you are in a transitional and unstable period like moving away from home. There will be many groups in your life and each of them will have established behavioral norms to which you feel the need to comply in order to be accepted.

If the group norms involve alcohol use then there is immediate pressure to drink.

In the specific case of a drinking culture, the group norms are often not specific or overt. It's not like joining the army where rules, behavioral norms and rank are clearly spelled out but they exist just as strongly even if they are never formally identified. If the girls are on a night out and the norm is to drink heavily then there is a decision to make. If you want to remain a part of the group and be popular and liked then you will also drink heavily and in doing so will create an expectation that will also drive future alcohol-related behavior.

When I made this change to my life, to stop drinking so heavily, I had to closely examine my friendships and social groupings and be honest with myself about what bound them together. Some of these relationships and the interactions they promoted were clearly alcohol-orientated in that heavy drinking was always a part of them.

In assessing how much I wanted or needed these friendships, I went through a process of identifying other beneficial aspects of the relationships within these social groupings besides the drinking. In some cases there just weren't any. When this was the case I just ended them. For others it was more difficult because many longer term friendships had more than alcohol as the glue that held them together, even though the drinking part had grown disproportionately as time had passed.

I felt that true friends would meet me halfway with the changes I wanted to make in my life, particularly as there were other aspects to the relationship. One of the disappointments for me of making my life change was that this didn't happen to quite the degree I had hoped for.

Trying to retain the valuable parts of a friendship whether that is with individuals or groups was trickier than I had thought it would be. In fact, I'm still working on the problem several years on. It may be that my change was more difficult for others than I had realized. I didn't handle some aspects of these relationship issues very well and that's something I have learned from. Perhaps I expected more than it was possible to give. But despite these difficulties other relationships were strengthened; particularly with my wife and on balance far more good than bad came from my decision.

Nowadays, it isn't so much of an issue because the social groups that survived and the ones that newly formed just accept that I don't drink much. At parties and social gatherings for example, friends often get some non-alcoholic beer in for me. What was once seen as a significant change is now accepted as me being me. I find this a pleasant and comfortable place to be.

Whenever you make changes to your life as significant as removing alcohol from it, other things will invariably change as well. Be prepared to face these challenges and give yourself time to adjust. It is important to realize that a relationship has two sides to it and you must not forget to consider the effect that your changed behavior will have on others.

Anaesthetizing

I often see people in my therapy practice who drink too much at home alone, perhaps concealing this behavior from others so nobody else could even suspect there may be a problem. The behavior may also take the form of drinking alone in a public place before or after social events or maybe a part of a daily routine. The singleton can just as easily hide in a packed bar as they can locked in their bedroom. Often they express a concern that, although they don't get drunk to the extent of losing control, they worry that their alcohol intake is consistently more than it should be. What might be the primary motivation for these solitary consumption patterns? Does it matter whether or not it's the more 'acceptable' half a bottle of wine at night or the striking dose of a bottle of vodka before lunch? What need does this solitary drinking behavior satisfy?

Accepting the premise that behavior is displayed for a reason and that it 'works' to alleviate uncomfortable underlying feelings then the reason becomes a critical part of the equation. The worst of these feelings can be effectively anaesthetized by the alcohol which then creates an oasis of tolerable emotion. It's odd how drinking alcohol can be as much a celebration as commiseration. That the desire to open a bottle of wine and finish it can be driven as much by the elation of a success as it can the disappointment of a failure.

Loneliness is a driver of excessive drinking behavior. It is not simply a reflection of nobody being around to enjoy a drink with, but the inner loneliness of the individual. When that feeling of being completely alone in your life is strong, a sense of isolation, insignificance and worthlessness often prevails.

My approach introduces the possibility of complete correction, 'cure', call it what you will. In my view, if the causes are removed then the addiction will collapse.

Isn't it just a physical thing?

So what is it then that causes someone to develop a problem with alcohol even at the expense of their closest relationships and their sense of stability? There is undoubtedly a reason for this behavior. Many explain it away in physiological terms, but in my experience, it is usually something within your belief system about yourself that causes you to abuse alcohol whilst others do not, but it often isn't easily identifiable. What appears on the surface is just a desire to drink, a craving. It might show up as a need to celebrate a job well done or it might be justified as solace for a bad day, or a comfort, something to help you sleep. It will invariably form around a need to negate bad feelings and make you feel better for that brief time until cold, hard reality looms again.

Look closely at what has just been said and note the words: 'craving', 'solace',' comfort', 'negate' and 'feel'. They all relate to emotions people feel or are emotions themselves. It is quite clear to me that the compulsion to drink heavily is driven by emotional needs.

For balance let's just recap what else might be going on.

Could it be the substance itself that creates the problem? Could it be encoded in your genes? Could you be already programmed to be susceptible to addiction and alcohol just happens to be the drug of choice?

My work supports a growing understanding that far from being a prisoner of your physiology you have the power to change it. Starting from the premise that people drink excessively for a reason or reasons and that eliminating them will permanently remove the need, it only remains to find out what these reasons are and then to construct a methodology to resolve them.

However alcohol does have physical effects and can create an altered balance in the body. In heavy, regular drinkers a physical dependency to the substance can develop. Because the body, over time, adapts to the excessive quantities of alcohol consumed, it does have to re-balance itself when intake is reduced or ceases completely. For those that are dependent, abrupt cessation of intake can be severe and dangerous if not managed properly. However not everyone experiences withdrawal symptoms to any distressing degree.

This 'correction' process doesn't last forever and any physical symptoms of withdrawal are relatively short lived. Long term alcoholism and relapse, therefore, are not explained by physical dependency alone.

Similarly the genetic model cannot fully account for our current understanding of what controls behavior. Bruce Lipton[4] has shown that such traits cannot possibly be solely genetic. This is partly because genes cannot switch themselves on or off.

The overwhelming evidence is that we are who we become primarily because of social and other environmental factors and not genetic make-up. This doesn't mean that you don't get your behavior from your parents, because you most certainly do, but it is mainly through learned experience rather than being embedded in the 'unalterable' gene passed directly to you at conception.

The beliefs and 'truths' that you record in your early years that get reinforced as your life progresses clearly shape the person you become.

From birth to around six years of age the human child unquestioningly records much of what it will need to know in order to survive in the society into which it has been introduced. Critical in this mix of information that becomes the child's core belief structure is the development of a sense of self and identity. What you truly believe about yourself is recorded in these early years and reinforced throughout your life by events and circumstances that support these fundamental beliefs. Happenings that oppose them are all but ignored.

Challenging the concept of genetic determinism

If a truth can be uncomfortable, it is that the more we discover about genetics the clearer it becomes how little we know. There are so many answers now being sought to what were at one time not even questions. Science, in many of its forms, has repeatedly proclaimed that the answer has been found, only to discover it is in error.

From the certainty of the Earth as the center of the universe to the unfolding of the human genome, science and scientists have had one thing in common and that is that they were all wrong in some aspect. Yet the process of scientific advancement relies on the continuing proposal and destruction of hypothesis. Few hypotheses are completely correct yet many hold a partial truth. It is by these means that discovery moves forward.

Genes and genetics fall into this category. Once the gene was discovered it was seen as having all the answers. Watson and Crick[5] discovered the double helix form of DNA and having achieved this breakthrough, as the story goes, they walked into the Eagle pub in Cambridge, and Crick announced: "We have found the secret of life!"[6]

That was 1953. Years later, all we know for sure is that we haven't yet discovered the secret of life. It appears to be considerably more complicated than was initially thought. Until recently genetic determinism still held centre stage. The idea that DNA controls most aspects of behavior was represented in most medical text books as the 'central dogma', arguing the 'primacy of DNA' right up to the end of the last century and in many cases beyond. This isn't just untrue but it has left a belief in its wake that the world will have difficulty in moving away from. One of the areas where this is the case is in the search for behavioral and physical disorders in human beings. Who hasn't heard of the cancer gene, the diabetes gene or the obesity gene? It's often argued that genes are responsible for behavior or illness whereas they may only be 'associated' with them. The widespread lay perception of a genetic causation can often be counterproductive, depleting ones sense of personal power by providing a convenient excuse.

Epigenetics or 'control above genes', is a relatively new concept that undermines this belief in genetic determinism. Epigenetic research has established that DNA blueprints passed on are not set in stone and can be changed by the influence of the environment including nutrition and emotions. It is argued that the chromosomal proteins in a cell can play as much of a part in cellular inheritance as the genes themselves. Genes determine height, color of eyes and hair in a clear cut fashion but not illness or behavior in the unalterable way we have been led to believe they do, with a few key exceptions. It is true though that the root causes of behavior and physical malfunctions may well be passed from parent to child but with rare exceptions it is not via the genes alone.

Epigenetics studies show that there can be as many as 30,000 different variations of proteins[7] that can be manufactured from the one gene blueprint. It appears that it isn't just the gene itself but how it is 'read' that affects the differences in outcome. The cellular environment, it seems, plays a major role in this complex process of protein production. The study of Epigenetics is moving us forward in the search for a better understanding of how this happens.

A phenomenal fact is that the genetic structure of mice and men is almost identical. Both of us have around 30,000 genes and we share 99% of them.

"We have only 300 unique genes in the human (genome) that aren't also in a mouse," said Craig Venter, president of Celera Genomics, the Maryland firm that led one of the mapping teams for the human genome project. "This tells me that genes can't possibly explain all of what makes us what we are."[8]

There doesn't seem to be enough capacity in the remaining gene pool to account for the millions of differences between us, so something else must be at play. At the moment that 'something else' is not clearly understood.

Whilst it isn't known exactly what makes us who we are, it is certain that genetic inheritance alone is not solely responsible for our behavior.

Challenging the concept of genetic determinism is very important because such a model fosters a sense of helplessness by engendering a belief that you can't do anything about it. It serves as a fantastic excuse to avoid making a change. If you buy into this model you can argue that it's just the way you are made and persuade yourself that you cannot do anything about the addiction other than fight it for the rest of your life.

Unfortunately helplessness is a dominant feature of conventional approaches. Understanding that your behavior is neither purely chemical nor genetic but primarily emotionally-driven does mean that you can re-establish a sense of control. You can decide to become involved in the process. Intention and involvement are prerequisites to success. You have to want to change your relationship with alcohol and address the beliefs that underpin it. If the negative emotions that are driving the excess drinking can be removed completely the addiction can be ended forever.

Summary

People drink heavily for a reason but they rarely understand what it is. It's self evident that if there was no reason to drink excessively it wouldn't happen.

The traditionally accepted approaches do not tend to address the reasons why people turn to drink.

There are a few key psychological themes that underlie drinking behavior and these need to be considered and explored. Although physiology obviously plays a part it is, in my view, overemphasized. The real work involves targeting the underlying emotions and beliefs.

Chapter 5

The power of belief

What controls behavior?

Current understanding about what makes us who we are shows that our perceptions have an enormous influence on our being. We are starting to appreciate how we function according to how we see the outside world.

A perception is a particular view of reality, in that you may see things differently from others. Our perceptions, therefore, are founded on the beliefs we hold about reality.

The science behind this is beautifully explained in Bruce Lipton's groundbreaking work *The Biology of Belief*. The essence of this work, which is now accepted by many, is that belief plays a much larger role in human behavior than had previously been thought.

We are what we believe. Henry Ford once stated "If you think you can do a thing or you think you can't do a thing, you're right". Einstein argued "Reality is merely an illusion, albeit a very persistent one". The role of our belief system is paramount in determining who we are and how we behave.

For me it was important that a connection could be made between the physicality of biological functions and the somewhat intangible mind. In the body we have observable and measurable behavior but the mind generates thought, perceptions and beliefs that are less well defined. Bruce Lipton's work furthers our understanding of what controls cellular function. As we are made up of communities of cells, understanding the behavior of the whole relies on an accurate appreciation of what is going on at a cellular and genetic level.

The realization that the control of cellular function wasn't solely dependent upon DNA began to shift our understanding. For this reason, it's helpful to explain briefly what it was he discovered because it will help you to better appreciate how powerful your belief system really is.

The 'Biology of Belief'

Lipton explains that there are cellular communities within the body that collectively perform the functions we need to thrive. The control of this cellular behavior, however, comes from the outside of the cells themselves. Cells are directed by signals from the environment. The signals are received by receptors on the cell membrane, the part that separates the external environment from the aqueous interior. These signals are chemical, electrical and energy based. The chemical and electrical signals generated are quite well understood but more recently it is thought there are also cell receptors that respond to energy waves from outside the body. It seems that a cell within the body has the capacity to respond to the external environment as well as the internal one.

Inside the cell resides the nucleus, previously thought to be the command center, which primarily contains the DNA and RNA. Each cell can be perceived as a fully functional organism in its own right with mini-organs (called organelles). These organize into an excretory system, skeletal system and nervous system just like the body as a whole.

On receiving an appropriate signal the cell performs an action which collectively results in a function being performed by the organism as a whole. This complex and beautiful operation is what causes your finger to move when you decide to lift it.

DNA resides in the nucleus of each cell. The early thinking held that the command structure of the cell must be here also because of the presence of DNA. It was thought that the nucleus was the 'brain' of the cell. On this basis, if a cell is enucleated (the nucleus removed) the cell should die. At the very least it should be incapable of functioning properly but, contrary to this expectation, Lipton showed that nothing much changes. The cell works and performs every bit as well as it did before except in its ability to replicate proteins. Of course the cell will die eventually because there is no DNA blueprint to build new parts when the existing ones wear out.

The results of the Human Genome project support these conclusions because that showed there just isn't enough DNA to explain the complexities of human behavior.

The project was a 13 year endeavor completed in 2003 whose goal was to identify all the genes in human DNA (genome) and determine the sequence of all 3 billion base pairs that make up the genome.

In order to account for the entire range of human behavior it was expected that there would be about 120,000 genes, yet only 24,000 were found. This suggests that the role DNA plays in the control of behavior is likely to be much less than previously thought.

This new understanding poses big questions for the science world, particularly with respect to the triggers of autoimmune illness. It redirects the focus to the outside, to our perceptions and underpinning these, our belief system.

Beliefs in the context of alcoholism

The subconscious part of our mind is the powerhouse of our belief system, that which makes each one of us who we are. It defines our identity by controlling our behavior in order that it complies with what is specified by our core beliefs. Although these fundamental and character forming beliefs control how we feel and determine our resultant behavior they are often false. Given this, absolute truth is questionable because it is often self-justifying. To an individual a belief is a truth. Behavior is displayed accordingly.

The adoption of personal truths (or beliefs) begins certainly at birth and possibly before. The newborn watches and learns; it understands love and anger, softness and harshness. This learning forms the framework of rules and personal truths that it will call upon time and time again to decide how to behave or react to situations. Perhaps how to respond to sudden changes in plans? How to act when under threat and generally how to live and thrive in the society into which it has been born? This recording of experience is uncritical and happens unchecked until critical evaluation abilities begin to develop at around the age of six or seven.

The brain filters reality based upon previous experience or already formed beliefs. Once the brain has learned what is right and 'true' it won't automatically address the accuracy or truth of that again. It functions rather like a computer program. It doesn't re-evaluate each time it is required to respond to a similar stimulus, it just does what it did last time. So what happens if some of these 'truths' aren't really true? What if they are completely wrong? What about experiences that have been misinterpreted and given the status of absolute truth?

A key feature of our belief system is that it will hear, see, understand and acknowledge that part of the outside world that already fits in with its general philosophy, and similarly, it will disregard that information which doesn't.

I cite a simple example, something that has happened to me on many occasions. Every few years it's time to change my car. I'm not particularly interested in cars or driving, I regard the whole personal transportation thing as a rather boring necessity. I couldn't tell you what make the car in front of me or behind me was because I have absolutely no interest in the subject. Things change, however, when it's time to buy a new one. All of a sudden I see the particular make of car that I'm thinking about everywhere. Car recognition has been raised in my perceptual radar whereas before it didn't feature.

The same thing happens with our core beliefs; perceptions that validate them are highly visible and the ones that don't aren't.

So what happens when it is a belief about our self? What if it is a belief that limits us in some way?

In this process of adopting the rules of life, these 'absolute truths' by which we have to live are all powerful in their influence upon how we feel and behave. They define our perception of ourselves in critical areas and they determine our behavior. Common dysfunctional beliefs about self include "I'm not good enough", "I'm not clever enough", "I have to be perfect to be loved", "I'm not pretty / strong / healthy etc" and the list goes on.

These beliefs are the result of an uncritical evaluation of the world outside and consequently are often wrong. The events that created the belief in the first place could easily have been misread. Most people I have worked with find their issues lessened when their core beliefs were challenged and modified.

Imagine the scenario of a young child listening to parents loudly arguing downstairs.

There may be no understanding of language but the emotions contained within the voices are clear. What is the child to make of it? The real reason for the conflict might be money or drinking or some other issue between the adults and it probably won't relate to the child, but how does the child know that? How can the child understand things of which it has no knowledge? One of the fundamental duties of the brain is to make sense of the outside world in all its forms, so whatever is occurring will be perceived by the child and ascribed a meaning using the limited under-standing it has. It simply cannot be meaningless to the devel-oping human brain. A child might typically assume that the problem somehow relates to its relationship with the parents and consequently there is nothing preventing the child from concluding that they themselves have done something wrong.

How is a four year old girl going to understand why her father is leaving home for good? She has no concept of infidelity or abuse or the other adult reasons for an acrimonious split. She does know about her relationship with her father however. Her limited knowledge may easily result in an incorrect interpretation of what is happening in order for her brain to make some sense of it. She might conclude, for example, that "if Daddy really loved me he wouldn't leave me".

In this example there is ample opportunity for the undeveloped mind of the child to conclude that they are involved and perhaps in some way to blame. The formations of beliefs about self worth are beginning to take shape. Events that support these early beliefs will strengthen them and those that oppose the belief will be ignored.

Incorrect and limiting beliefs about one's self will affect feelings and behavior throughout adult life.

For the drinker there is also the comfort of having established a drinking identity. "I'm a drinker, therefore I drink". It is a part of who they are. Something has to change to make 'not drinking' feel comfortable. If the drinking were to be radically reduced new and often difficult challenges would present in a number of areas and they are likely to unsettle the balance.

Using willpower alone to try to redefine one's identity is destined to fail in the long term. This is because serious internal conflict results when one tries to act in a way that opposes fundamental core beliefs about self. The emotional desire to drink continues to be generated.

If the beliefs are addressed then change can occur without resistance.

Many argue that overcoming the dependent state is the main hurdle. However, the physical discomfort associated with coming off alcohol is temporary and certainly not the main problem in conquering an 'addiction'. If the challenge was merely getting over the dependence, nobody would 'fall off the wagon'. Once detoxified that should be it, yet people often relapse suggesting that something else is driving the behavior.

It's not easy to change beliefs consciously as changes usually have to be made at the subconscious level to last. People do things for a reason and addicts indulge because it serves a function. It isn't crazy or inexplicable, it's logical and understandable. People with substance misuse problems have good reasons to persist with their behavior despite knowing it is damaging them.

Changing core beliefs

For permanent behavioral change the underlying emotions and the core beliefs that sustain the dysfunction have to be addressed at the subconscious level. Hypnosis and EFT appropriately targeted are two well established and very effective methods of stimulating such subconscious change.

They focus on emotional and behavioral issues and create change by identifying and processing the underlying causes. It has been postulated that it isn't just dysfunctional behavior that is rooted in core beliefs but that illnesses and disease may also follow the same pattern. So it follows that, potentially, physical illness may respond in some positive way to this form of intervention. EFT, in particular, is an effective tool at removing the negative emotional charge associated with the events that support and reaffirm the problematic core beliefs. How you feel about yourself, your life and your relationships at the subconscious level will affect your behavior and your susceptibility to alcohol or other mind altering substances.

Summary

Our behavior is driven by what we believe and, in particular, those fundamental beliefs we hold about ourselves. These beliefs are embedded in our subconscious and cannot easily be changed by conscious effort alone.

There are effective tools that help to make changes at a deep level that really do work when given an honest and open chance to do so.

One thing is clear......'We are what we believe".

Part 2 - Tools and techniques

What are we actually trying to do?

Treatment can either be conceptualized as a cure or as ongoing management. It seems that you can either fix something or control it. Fixing the problem really speaks for itself. Having to 'control' alcoholism requires constant vigilance, often ultimately, together with total abstinence.

It is better to aim to be truly ambivalent towards alcohol rather than fighting it indefinitely. Removing the underlying emotional reasons driving the need also removes the compulsion. This program aims to transform your relationship with alcohol so that it is no longer an issue. It requires your involvement and understanding and it is an approach that works.

The conventional approach is to create strong reasons not to drink. It is the approach of Alcoholics Anonymous and its 12 step program, the Priory and other alcohol support organizations. It constantly reminds you of a looming threat and what would happen to you if you relapse - death, bankruptcy and destitution. It provides everlasting support to help you fight the addiction, day in and day out for the rest of your life. You might even find that you substitute an AA addiction for the alcohol one. One thing is clearly set in stone – you must never allow even a drop of alcohol to pass your lips because as soon as you do you will plunge once again into the depths of drunken despair.

The old adage "One drink is too many and a thousand not enough" encapsulates the conventional approach to treating alcoholism.

Personally, I simply don't agree that this is the only way. The conventional approach supports your conscious desire not to drink but does not address the fundamental causes. It is an approach that helps some and fails many. It fosters fear and averts relapse by establishing an ever present awareness of those powerful reasons not to drink. It guarantees that you will never be free of the curse because even if you never touch a drop again the fear that you might is ever present.

It is in reality a power struggle set in motion now and designed to last forever.

There are fundamental problems that explain why so many people relapse or 'fall off the wagon'. There is a reason why so many people experience cycles of abstinence followed by indulgence again and again until death intervenes. Many of those who manage to avoid relapse are plagued with the fear of it and some truly become free because, for them, many of the underlying causes will have been fortuitously eradicated alongside the suppression and support regime, not as a result of it.

If the underlying causes of the addictive behavior are left unattended they may even strengthen as a result of ongoing life experience and may grow to such an extent that they overshadow the opposing 'stay sober' agenda. When this happens relapse often occurs. The traumas in life are akin to emotional 'bombs', some small and some large, that can derail well intentioned sobriety. We all endure emotional turmoil in our lives from time to time and it is upsetting and challenging but for the abstaining alcoholic such events threaten their delicate internal balance of desire and fear. The combination of pre-existing unresolved negative emotions, together with a new traumatic event, can often derail a promising recovery. When this happens a return to the 'bottle' becomes ever more likely.

Either the powerful anti-drinking reasons can falter or the support might not be available when needed. For example, if illness and the fear of death formed a part of one's opposition to drinking, it may diminish if a terminal illness is diagnosed. "I'm going to die/get divorced/lose my job/some other bad thing, anyway so what's the point?"

The opposition reasons can be weakened in much the same way as the emotional drivers can be strengthened and unless these remain in homeostatic balance something will give.

Traditional approaches rarely intentionally and specifically remove the addiction problem completely, but they still hold value. Such intervention may be the only immediate and available way to avoid an imminent descent into oblivion. Sometimes it is necessary to fight the compulsion head on with an enforced abstinence regime, continuing support and perhaps medication but such an approach isn't a permanent solution even if it is an essential part of one. It may be necessary to intervene to get to a position where one is capable of addressing the underlying causes but for most, such drastic action isn't necessary.

The emotions that drive the addiction are usually not created in consciousness, rather they function at the subconscious level. This is why it is common for someone to rationally appreciate and be able to express a clear understanding of the fact that their drinking is excessive and damaging yet be unable to stop. By addressing the underlying reasons the relationship with alcohol changes and the problem clears permanently as if it had never existed. Failure to address underlying negative emotions and change the beliefs that support them, leaves one at the mercy of that delicate balance and the lifelong struggle it creates.

The techniques introduced in this chapter, Hypnotherapy and EFT, both help facilitate effective and lasting change at the subconscious level. EFT has the added advantage of being able to be used as a self-help tool.

Chapter 6

Hypnotherapy

What is hypnotherapy?

Hypnotherapy is the term used to describe the process of achieving behavioral change for an individual whilst they are in a deeply relaxed state. *Hypnosis* is the methodology used to induce the level of relaxation required. The 'therapy' part usually comprises of a series of suggestions delivered in such a way as to increase the probability that the person will integrate and act upon them at the subconscious level. As a result of these suggestions the behavior displayed is typically altered.

You can experience hypnotherapy either by going to a therapist or by listening to a pre-recorded session. The script used in a one-to-one session is usually tailored to the problem and in some cases written specifically for the client in question. Hypnotherapy recordings tend to be more general in nature.

Appendix 2 provides additional material with descriptions of my own recordings and details on how you can download them. In *Appendices 3 and 4* I have included the transcripts used on the recordings for your interest.

A typical hypnotherapy session would contain the following phases:

- Trance induction
- Deepening
- Suggestion (often involving the use of metaphor)
- Awakening

The trance state

The deeply relaxed state is sometimes called a 'trance', although many therapists prefer to describe it as 'deep relaxation' because it doesn't carry with it the same implication of losing control or having something done to you.

The ability to enter this deeply relaxed state varies from individual to individual. Some people find it easy to enter trance and others find it quite difficult. Because it depends on the individual person, try not to think of it as something the hypnotherapist does to you rather something you determine. The therapist simply acts as a facilitator.

About one person in five (20%) can enter this deep relaxed state quite quickly and will respond readily to 'direct' suggestion. Most people require a more gradual and subtle approach to the trance induction and more permissive and 'indirect' suggestions.

A deliberately induced trance state allows control of:

- Depth
- Duration
- Subject matter

Shifting awareness from the fully conscious state to a more relaxed and suggestible one is quite a natural transition and some people are able to do this without external input. All forms of hypnosis are essentially self-hypnosis but the effectiveness has been optimized by the refinement of trance inducing techniques over the years. These refinements primarily help people adopt suggestions that might otherwise be screened or critiqued by the conscious mind.

The trance state is actually a natural phenomenon and everyone experiences it on a regular basis, without necessarily realizing it. It happens in those moments just before going to sleep at night and that fleeting period on the point of waking up. It is that in-between zone when dreaming is still active and vivid just before conscious awareness returns. The pre-sleep transition is usually longer and holds more potential. It is often the time when good ideas seem to surface out of nowhere, when a novel tune or literary phrase emerges from the depths of your mind, or when exciting and innovative solutions to problems appear. Many recognize this phenomenon and some make use of it by waking and scribbling notes so that they can be reviewed and acted upon at a later time but most of us just allow them to pass. Sometimes we wish we had been more proactive as, commonly, by the morning, these insights have faded and any remaining detail is usually insufficient to be useful.

People can often also achieve a light trance when just daydreaming, doodling or passing a few moments quietly alone. Similarly intense involvement in a book engages the imagination and stimulates the same mind state as a deliberately induced trance. Music, particularly if it has a repetitive beat is very effective at inducing trance and often forms part of ritual induction processes. Hypnosis also aids this very natural ability we all have to focus inwardly, to meditate and contemplate quietly.

Open to suggestion

For long term success the desired behavioral change should come from the client, guided by the hypnotherapist, involving indirect rather than direct suggestion. Therapist driven direct suggestion may be met with resistance whereas allowing the client to come up with their own ideas is much more likely to be accepted at the subconscious level.

Hypnotic suggestions, whether direct or indirect, stand a better chance of being acted upon if the conscious part of the mind is set to one side to avoid critique, analysis and rejection. This is exactly what happens when the depth of relaxation reaches the trance state. Most people will enter a trance more easily if the process is indirect, unthreatening, progressive and gentle. Similarly they will respond better to suggestion if it is indirect, given through metaphor and when it doesn't offer a direct challenge to powerful subconscious beliefs.

A 'post hypnotic suggestion' is a form of 'direct' suggestion made to the client whilst they are in a hypnotic trance. It is designed to elicit a desired behavior or restrict an unhelpful one when they are awake and usually when it is only needed for a short time. An example might be "the next time you are asked to count to 10 you will completely forget about the number seven". Often this type of post hypnotic suggestion is used in stage hypnosis but can also be used to convince skeptical clients of the effects of subconscious suggestion.

To use direct or post hypnotic suggestion for long term behavioral change, most likely, wouldn't work. The suggestion "from today you will intensely dislike the taste of alcohol" will probably evaporate after a few hours.

Habit and the power of the subconscious

The size, power and multitasking capabilities of the subconscious mind are truly without comparison. The conscious mind often thinks it's in charge but defers all the really important stuff to that part of us that doesn't judge or question. It is in the subconscious that your core beliefs are held and emotional responses generated. The reason it is so difficult to change a behavior that you consciously know is damaging to you is because it is not under conscious control. It is the inner part of you that has to change and whilst that is possible, it cannot easily be done with willpower alone and requires a different approach to conscious rational exploration and resolution.

Consider all the things you do without conscious thought. Activities like walking, reading, driving and so on, all involve a subconscious element with the potential to exercise conscious control. Without this duality all of our time would be spent monitoring our basic functions and people would continually fall over or crash the car. Many routine daily activities require minimal conscious brain activity. Despite the obvious advantage of subconscious pre-programming, the major downside is the difficulty encountered changing behavior.

This applies to reading just as much as it does to drinking. When a new item is being learned there is considerable brain activity yet once learned, similar tasks simply utilize this knowledge and require very little additional mental processing. The brain has a stored record of what it needs to do and it can access this quickly and easily when required. It continues to perform learned tasks in this way until some new learning takes place and modifies the behavior.

When you next look at a sign or a newspaper headline, try to do it without actually reading it. It isn't possible for most of us because the skill has been learned and become automated. The same automatic processes are at play in other forms of learned behavior including drinking alcohol.

Some unwanted behaviors comprise a habitual component to a greater or lesser degree depending upon both the individual and the behavior. In most cases the habit will have to be addressed in its own right.

Conscious versus subconscious

The conscious part of our mind is only responsible for managing a very small part of our life experience. The capability of the subconscious mind is far greater.

To make changes to the subconscious you need more influence where it matters and your message has to make sense and speak the language this part of the mind responds to. Getting this balance right will help change fundamental beliefs about drinking.

Hypnosis can be viewed as having a direct line of communication to the subconscious mind. The subconscious has incomparable wisdom and sophistication and it knows which part of a story to take note of even if, consciously, you remain in the dark. It knows which suggestions being presented will be beneficial to you and is able to make the necessary changes immediately.

The conscious part of the mind is always present and is able to exert control if it wishes. When in trance it takes on the role of an observer, generally not interfering with the process though it could at any time and is more likely to if something interrupts the flow. The retention of some conscious awareness is the reason why people will not act or behave in a way that opposes their normal rational judgments as to what is appropriate and safe behavior and what is not.

It is equally true that people will not override their fundamental core beliefs, those things they hold to be absolutely true. They will not act in a way that significantly contradicts them without generating strong emotions that effectively limit their ability to comply with the process. One cannot be cajoled or tricked into acting in a way that directly opposes core principles. Everything that happens during this deeply relaxing process is with the permission, directly or indirectly, of the conscious mind.

Having entered trance it is quite possible for people to make very significant and instant changes to their behavior and feelings. I never cease being amazed by such dramatic and rapid change despite witnessing it over and over again. It is the process that enables people to quit smoking immediately and forever after having smoked 40 a day for 30 years, to lose weight and keep it off and to eliminate long standing fears and anxieties as if they had never existed. Of prime relevance is the ability of hypnotherapy to fundamentally change the way one feels about alcohol.

Neuro Linguistic Programming
The success of the hypnotic processes described above has been significantly aided through a greater understanding of how the mind interprets the spoken word. A number of additional techniques and modifications have been developed over the years to help people attain a sufficiently relaxed state and others

to help address long standing behavioral problems. Many of these are now considered to sit within the ever expanding realm of Neuro Linguistic Programming (NLP)[9].

Richard Bandler and John Grinder, the creators of NLP, analyzed and interpreted the patterns of speech used by Milton Erickson, the founding father of modern hypnotherapy, as a part of their development of the methodology.

At the time NLP was primarily concerned with how the brain interprets spoken words when they are combined together in a sentence, and what happens if some information, that one would normally expect to be there, is missing.

The effect of omissions or different groups of words spoken to people when in a trance state was also analyzed. When information that one would rightly expect to be there is missing from a sentence or, when something is said which is contradictory, the subconscious mind will still attempt to derive some meaning. The conscious mind also becomes confused and spends its time trying to work out a rational understanding and seems to relinquish, in part, its more usual critiquing role. This deliberate ambiguity causes the client's subconscious mind to conclude that which was initially desired by the therapist. It is as if it was the client's idea from the beginning.

It is brilliant in its simplicity. Just by structuring statements in a particular way the conscious mind can be diverted and the subconscious reprogrammed.

It is because of this specific use of language that non-native speakers of the language used by the therapist may not experience the same effect because the NLP language constructs rely upon native interpretation.

NLP now has a much broader scope. It embodies a wide range of techniques and the number continues to grow with new mechanisms emerging that serve to optimize the hypnotic process. Whilst this book isn't about the technicalities of NLP or its specific mechanisms, it's useful to have a basic understanding of the influence of language and some of the approaches used to help positive suggestion integrate more effectively and to help minimize conscious resistance.

Non-specific factors (including intention)

You should be aware that factors surrounding your decision to change can be effective alongside the formal therapy itself. Simply making the appointment, or making time available and going to a different place is highly influential. Allowing an unfamiliar process to unfold and interacting with a therapist you don't know are other non-specific factors that also have an effect. Making a space to deliberately focus on an issue, as well as expressing the intention to change can help to move things forward.

Even listening to a recorded hypnosis session at home confers many of the same advantages. The decision to buy it and then find a quiet and peaceful time to listen will quite naturally increase the effectiveness of the process.

We must acknowledge that thinking about a problem, having the intention to behave differently and doing 'something' about it may be as effective as the hypnosis itself.

When such intention is combined with creative hypnotic and suggestive techniques positive change is much more likely to occur.

I personally feel that intention is greatly undervalued. One of Gary Craig's[10] educational DVD's (Steps toward becoming the ultimate therapist) features a presentation by the Stanford University scientist Dr. William Tiller. Dr Tiller tells of the many experiments he conducted where material and measurable changes occurred to an electrical potential purely through the application of focused intention. No touching, just thinking. This is thought provoking in the extreme and supports the view that intention may be considerably more powerful than we hitherto have accepted.

I firmly support the view that intention to succeed can and will change your brain architecture. It will create new neural pathways and alter how you see yourself, your life and your role. To maintain such intention to change will help significantly.

Things don't always go to plan

Hypnotherapy isn't a panacea. It isn't completely successful for everyone. Some people don't respond as well as others for a variety of reasons. They may be anxious or preoccupied. There can be a fear of losing control. People's response can be influenced by the mood of the moment and other distracting issues that are active in their life at that time. Such anxiety limits the effectiveness of the therapy.

When people do not achieve the results they hoped for other factors are usually present. It may be that the individual is not ready for the change, the time might not be right or the unwanted behavior may serve too much of a protective function. Other techniques might need to be used to tackle this resistance. Whatever the reason for less than completely successful therapy using hypnosis it need not be permanent. A better understanding of hypnosis and how it works often helps to remove anxiety and can improve results, as does practice in deep breathing and any form of purposeful relaxation.

Summary

Hypnotherapy uses one's natural ability to deeply relax and offers suggestions in an unthreatening way to permanently change subconscious patterns.

The trance state is something we are all familiar with and its key function is that it increases suggestibility. There are various ways of inducing trance, some rapid and others slower and gentler. Suggestion can be direct or indirect, the latter often employing the use of metaphor.

Therapeutic hypnosis or hypnotherapy is usually permissive

in approach and is a well established way of inducing change at the subconscious level.

Addressing distorted beliefs around alcohol using hypnotherapy is more effective than consciously trying to fight these cravings.

Chapter 7

Emotional Freedom Techniques
(The Tapping Therapy)

I had seen Trevor once before, regarding his desire to quit smoking. On this second visit, his wife accompanied him as she wanted to have a brief discussion with me about her struggle to lose weight. So after we had completed the therapy session, all three of us sat down to talk.

I couldn't help noticing that she seemed to be in some discomfort with her hands so I asked her about it.

It transpired that she had suffered with arthritis in both hands for some time and, as is often the case, some days were more painful than others. Although there was visible minor disfigurement around some of the finger joints she could still use her hands more or less normally. Today was one of the more painful days and she had markedly restricted movement. She wanted to know if hypnosis could help her lose weight but my intuition prompted me to follow this initial line of enquiry before addressing this issue. I asked her which hand was more painful, where exactly the pain was and some details about its nature. I then led her through two rounds of tapping (EFT) and to her surprise the pain subsided before we reached the end of the second round.

She was now able to open and close her hands without discomfort. In less than four minutes a clear cut sensation of pain with a 'real' physical cause, together with the associated impairment, had gone completely. Free and easy movement returned.

She turned to her husband with a puzzled expression and said, "What did he do?"

I've seen many similar shifts with EFT before and when it's as profound as this, I am reminded of the immense power of our subconscious minds and the remarkable ability of this simple technique to harness this in some small way. I have little true understanding as to why these shifts occur. I cannot see inside and fully understand the mechanics of the physiology at play, so I cannot fully explain these phenomena. I can tell you that such changes do happen regularly and relatively consistently.

I relate this particular story to you, not because it is the most extreme or the most life changing case I've seen, but because it involved the resolution of observable symptoms which have a well established cause. The improvement occurred in minutes, required no chemical intervention and due to the temporal sequence of events it's highly unlikely that such a dramatic change could have been caused by anything else.

Now don't get me wrong, the relief she experienced didn't mean that the arthritis had miraculously resolved, or that she would never experience a similar pain again, but it does illustrate that feelings, including pain can respond positively to this procedure.

Although this example relates to the treatment of a physical symptom, EFT is more often associated with relieving emotional pain and related unwanted behavior. Alcohol misuse can be seen as an unwanted behavior driven by negative emotions. EFT is used to uncover and collapse these by breaking the connection between long past events and emotions that are still attached to them. Unlike arthritis or toothache, where the pain has a clear and current source, emotional pain can remain long after the events that initially created it and often the connections are not so obvious.

In my view, as is probably clear by now, the primary driving force behind substance abuse including alcohol is emotional. The emotions are the result of conflicting realities between the core beliefs you hold about yourself and the image that society dictates you ought to be. The source of the beliefs that create such emotional pain often track back to childhood and parental relationships. Whilst later life traumas may stimulate those emotions or bring them to the surface, the root causes generally lie within those early formations of belief about life and self. Despite the fact that they are long standing and powerful they can be changed.

The effect of using EFT may be seen as direct observable change, as in the example above, or a less easily definable change, for example, a reduction in the level of emotional intensity around a specific issue.

Despite the fact that Trevor did quit smoking – and I saw him on a number of business related occasions for many months after where I could confirm that – his wife didn't return for treatment of any kind, so perhaps this strange happening was scary in some way, or perhaps she just didn't fancy the journey. I don't know why she didn't return to work on her weight issues but these things happen and I just put it down to one more thing I don't fully understand.

What I can derive from the event was that a significant change occurred to a sensation of pain that was caused by arthritis. A dramatic shift from intense discomfort to a complete pain-free state in less than four minutes – and not a drug in sight!

What is EFT?

Emotional Freedom Techniques is a body-based psychotherapy that involves repetitive tapping on sensitive points on the body in order to process memory or discharge emotion.

It can be self applied or used in a therapy context.

EFT was developed and brought to the world by an American engineer, Gary Craig[10]. It grew out of another tapping therapy called 'Thought Field Therapy' (TFT)[11]. Both of these purport to effect change in the body's bio-energetic system (or thought field) as understood in Traditional Chinese Medicine.

Energy is believed to flow through a number of invisible channels called 'meridians' and any disturbance, emotional or physical, is thought to relate to a disruption of this flow. In both EFT and TFT each point relates to a different meridian which in turn has a specific connection to bodily organs and an association with different emotions.

For example the point under the eye is thought to be the start point of the stomach meridian and tapping on it is particularly helpful at reducing anxiety or fear as well as cravings, which are forms of anxiety.

The relationship between a tapping point, a meridian and a client problem is highly relevant in TFT where specific tapping routines are designed to match the client's issues. The philosophical change that Gary Craig introduced was to ignore point specifity to all intents and purposes and work on all the meridians in a standard sequence regardless of the presenting problem. The process he developed was so quick to apply that distinguishing between the meridians, their associated organs and emotional connections took longer than working with all of them at the same time.

A 'round' of tapping became a standardised process of cycling through all the main points in the same sequence. Each re-application just repeats the same cycle. It makes the whole process more integrated and easier to learn and apply. One effect of this simplification is to make self application much easier. Rather than remain a predominantly therapist-applied process, with complex algorithms supplied to order (as is the case in TFT), the simplification embodied in EFT creates more opportunities for people to help and treat themselves with minimal training.

Stimulating points on the body is not a new idea. The concept of energy flow in the body through specific channels with multiple access points is the foundation for Acupuncture, a treatment that has been around in various forms for some time. The first written account of the structure of meridians and 'energy flow' appeared in a Chinese document known as Shiji, probably written between 109 BC and 91 BC.[12]

How does it work?

Whether the positive results achieved with EFT are really due to the tapping on energy meridians or the effects are due to other specific or non-specific factors (including conditioning, neuro-transmitter release, or the placebo effect) is not entirely clear and requires further study. It does seem to be true, however, that the process as a whole exerts a potent effect.

The body uses an electrical as well as a biochemical system to communicate between the multi-cellular communities within. Modern medical, as opposed to surgical, interventions, for all their benefits, are generally focused upon the biochemical system and the electrical system. The interest in the electrical system tends to be wholly centered on visible nerve pathways. The search for cures of the ills of today pays virtually no attention to the body's more elusive bio-energetic system. Partly as a result of the considerable influence of the pharmaceutical industry, modern medicine is primarily concerned with exploring ways to increase the scope of chemical intervention with the inevitable consequence of producing more and more drugs.

The accepted view of our society is that disciplines working predominantly with the body's chemistry are considered 'mainstream' and are restricted to formally qualified medical practitioners. Individuals that work with 'energy' are usually described as 'alternative,' don't require any formal medical qualifications and are considered by many within the estab-lishment to be 'unscientific'.

Why isn't there more study on the body's ability to heal itself?

It is interesting to note that the conventional response to a 'medically impossible' recovery is dismissal. As these occurrences are not easily explained by the medical model there is an element of denial that tends to kick in. They are not generally regarded as sufficiently significant to warrant further investigation and cases are often dismissed as having been an incorrect diagnosis in the first place. Sometimes this happens with cancer patients who just get better after they have already been written off.

Uncomfortably for the establishment, unexpected recovery also occurs with patients in drug trials who are given the placebo and not the drug itself but this information, as you might expect, isn't of primary interest to the drug companies who often sponsor the trials, so it isn't overly emphasized.

The 'placebo effect' is the term used to describe an improvement in a medical condition or symptom after the application of an inactive compound in place of the active preparation when the subject believes it to be the actual medication. In double blind studies the placebo preparation is made to look and taste exactly like the medication and the staff administering it are 'blinded', that is they too have no idea whether it is the medication or not. Everything about the process is identical except that the tablet contains no drug at all.

With this in mind you might think that people who manage to completely cure themselves of these life threatening conditions would be worthy of further investigation, that perhaps the placebo effect conceals more than the rather neutral word suggests. You might also think that in drug trials where the placebo outperforms the active drug, some effort might be directed towards understanding these remarkable phenomena, yet on the whole that doesn't seem to be the case. There are often other agendas at play.

For various reasons accurate and comprehensive figures are sometimes difficult to get from drug trials but it is clear that instances of self healing or unexplained recovery happen much more often than is generally thought. Viewed individually they can easily be put down to unknown and immaterial causes, but if analyzed collectively, they might provoke some discomfort in those that don't consider belief to be a potent and relevant factor.

Chronic disorders, particularly those with an auto immune element, e.g. diabetes, some forms of cancers and heart disease etc. are poorly managed in the western world. The modern day approach is symptom management rather than seeking to address the underlying cause. This approach happens to be the most financially beneficial for the pharmaceutical industry.

The incidence of breast cancer in the UK grew by over 70% between 1971 and 2001[13]. Medical treatment has improved markedly for this type of cancer and when screening was intro-duced it had a significant effect. If it's diagnosed early enough and a treatment regime put in place, there is every possibility that eventual death will not be as a result of the disease. However, as the mortality rate has only declined by 5% between 1950 and 2003 advancements in the management of the disease aren't keeping up. For some other conditions the outlook is even bleaker. Despite the fact that we are not winning the battle there is little likelihood of a change in direction.

Medical research costs money and currently, in much of the world, that money comes from the sale of drugs. Without finance there is little hope for the funding of research into the workings of the body's energy system (whatever that is) and the ability of the mind to correct physical malfunctions. There are many alter-native therapy modalities that exist. Acupuncture, homeopathy and hypnosis are some of the better known ones. There are multiple organizations representing these therapies and even within the same discipline they often cannot unite and agree on a way forward. I suspect that at the moment, the alternative therapy scene as a whole is too fragmented and disorganized to drive a change in direction.

The evidence for EFT

Tapping therapies including EFT have traditionally been based on the presumed existence of 'energy meridians' as described earlier and the assumption that the energy flow within the body is critically important to its wellbeing. Acupuncture, for example, is well established and almost considered to be a mainstream therapy despite the continued difficulty in providing unequivocal evidence as to the existence of meridians and descriptions of the flow of energy within them.

Some things can be measured. The body does generate an electrical current which is measurable and there have been a few small publications supporting the existence of meridian channels.[14] In addition there is some evidence that acupuncture points differ from surrounding skin in terms of electrical conductivity and receptor density. However, conclusive proof of the energy system remains elusive.

Perhaps a more important question might be, "Does it really matter that much?"

However unscientific it is, the evidence, for me, of the success of EFT is embodied within my own experience. When I started using the approach some years ago I was excited by the anecdotes of individuals and the testaments of other therapists as to the effectiveness and speed with which long term issues could be resolved.

When I began introducing the techniques to my clients I saw directly the benefits they could achieve.

The medical establishment employs techniques such as 'double blind studies' to prove the efficacy of an intervention however 'energy' therapies have been the subject of few high quality studies. There are a handful of randomised controlled studies looking at EFT but their size and quality are not optimal though a considerable amount of anecdotal evidence exists supported by thousands of case studies published on the internet. There are also some systematic reviews on energy-based psychology models including those by Phil Mollon in the UK and David Feinstein in the US.

High quality research in this area could broaden acceptance of this useful approach. Firstly the emphasis must be on establishing beyond doubt that the processes work and for what problems are they best suited, then the focus should move on to addressing the question of how they work. The creation of a proven alternative to our drug obsessed society would have many benefits but significant political and financial obstacles remain.

Whether an energy system other than the central nervous system exists or not is difficult to prove. The universe uses other energies such as magnetism and gravity, the true nature of which remain mysterious and there are clearly many things we don't understand. Perhaps there are other forces out there that we have not yet learnt to measure.

The power of the mind in creating personal change should not be underestimated and the influence of concepts such as intention and techniques involving visualization, both prominent features of EFT, may play a greater part in our wellbeing than is presently acknowledged. It could be that all the alternative therapies just represent different routes to the same common pathway.

Using EFT

There are a number of talking therapies including psychoanalysis and Cognitive Behavioral Therapy (CBT) that have been shown to have benefits but typically seem to take longer to exert their influence than EFT. Some issues are complex and can take time, sometimes years, but because EFT inherently promotes self application, people can continue to work on their problems independently and formal therapy sessions can be significantly reduced. Counseling over the phone with EFT can also be highly effective which adds to the flexibility of its practical application.

Some issues resolve quite quickly and others take more time but the speed of resolution often doesn't seem to be related to the presenting problem but appears to be more dependent on the individual themselves. Whether the problem is alcohol dependency or obesity the underlying cause is often structured along the same lines. The unwanted behavior is usually the result of a subconscious choice. It may be alcohol, drugs or food and there are those who mix and match. It just depends on what's available and acceptable within an individual's life.

The work with EFT is to identify and collapse those negative emotions and amend or overwrite the beliefs that create them. Behavior then tends to follow suit. An important factor is how the individual has processed and integrated events from the past. It is these emotional residues from past events that remain in the subconscious part of the mind and tend to cause problems. The resultant behavior is often a desperate attempt to manage these powerful needs.

It is my view that the combination of tapping whilst maintaining focus on emotional distress surrounding past events changes the way people feel about the event and themselves more quickly and more consistently than other more traditional and accepted approaches.

What do you actually do?
The following pages explain the EFT process and show you the points to be used. How to apply the tapping to your alcohol problem forms part of the later program section, but the details of where and how to tap, how often and how to measure results are included below in order that you can practice using the procedure, working on any issue you would like to address. This might be a headache, a wheezy chest or perhaps an anxiety about meeting new people. When practicing, focus on the issue as closely as you can. When learning EFT, try not to choose issues that are likely to stir you up too much. Focus on stand-alone

emotions and physical symptoms that are not obviously connected to past traumatic events.

I've met quite a few people who have chosen to attend EFT training courses at Level 1 and Level 2 specifically to improve their understanding of the techniques for personal benefit. Many find that immersing themselves in a training environment significantly increases their proficiency with EFT because close interaction with others accelerates the learning process.

General tapping guidance

- Tap at least seven times on each point before moving to the next one in the sequence.
- Tap firmly but not enough to hurt or bruise.
- Use as many fingers as you like (I've suggested a number in the photos). It doesn't matter which hand you choose to tap with.
- Stay focused on the issue, (emotions/physical symptoms) not the process
- Where points are bi-lateral it doesn't matter which side you use

Targeting 'aspects'

Negative emotions include anxiety, depression, anger, addictive cravings, fears and phobias. These emotions support and drive unwanted behavior. Pain, though not obviously recognizable as an emotion, has many similar aspects and as described earlier, responds positively to EFT.

EFT often collapses negative emotions. These emotions are current but are often activated by subconscious memories of past events, even when the memory in question is not consciously recalled. Tapping will usually reduce the emotional intensity but it may also cause the surfacing of a different emotion still connected with the event.

I once worked with a client who had an extremely distressing experience during the birth of her child. The episode, for her, was devastating. The birth was exceptionally painful and she felt very poorly treated by the hospital. It left her feeling as if she were, in her words, just a piece of meat. The story of the birth was freely given during the initial counseling phase with no display of emotion when talking about it. It felt as if this event had already been processed by her, that it was something she had dealt with. It seemed that, whilst it was traumatic, the emotional connection had been severed.

It turns out that she was able to speak of this event rationally because she had found an internal mechanism to suppress the emotions surrounding it, however further tapping revealed that painful emotions were still firmly connected and were, in part, responsible for the issues she was struggling with in the present. Although the emotions influencing her current life were firmly connected with this event, the link was not consciously apparent. Even if it had been, the coping mechanism she developed masked the importance so as to make it appear inert.

Usually negative emotions manifest when unprocessed distressing events are explored. During the counseling part of the process clients are asked how they feel in the present, what feelings they generally have when they choose to drink, when this last happened and can they remember how they felt then. This gentle exploration often reveals some current emotional intensity around certain themes. Tapping is then gently introduced whilst recapping what has just been explored and the currently active emotion often changes or subsides uncovering other emotions and other memories, each with their own level of intensity. Typically this layered process continues until each important aspect of the problem is addressed and resolved.

It may be that anger targeted at someone else is really a defense against more personal emotions and fears and it is by this mechanism that the more damaging emotions remain subconsciously shielded by the superficial façade of anger. Collapsing the anger may reveal an underlying emotion which in turn may expose yet another level beneath. In the session transcript at the end of this chapter you will see this for yourself - the initially angry response from the client was shielding feelings of guilt. It isn't unusual for such superficial feelings to be directed at others in order to provide protection against more personal ones.

Dysfunctional or incorrect core beliefs are typically supported by many of life's events. Some of these will be so small as to be insignificant and others will be highly influential in maintaining, confirming and reinforcing these invalid beliefs. As there can often be more than one emotion associated with a past event there can also be more than one event supporting the underlying belief. In EFT terms the various memory clips of an event and the negative emotions, physical symptoms and unhelpful beliefs connected to it are called 'aspects'. Stripping away the layers of aspects as they emerge will eventually collapse the invalid and wrong belief in its entirety. When such wrong beliefs are collapsed all the feelings and subsequent behaviors they were supporting also go.

It isn't necessary to uncover and collapse all of the aspects supporting a behavioral condition because it has been shown that after a number of them have been resolved the remainder will naturally clear. This is known as the 'generalization effect' and is a phenomenon shared with other therapies.

You might imagine a belief to be a table with six legs. It isn't necessary to remove every leg before the table falls. If one initially selects only the most important legs, perhaps only two or three have to be removed for it to fall.

For each negative emotion that emerges it is important to calibrate the degree to which the emotion is being felt. One has to know how severe or intense the emotion is when it first surfaces and then again after the application of a few rounds of EFT. The measurement used to calibrate is called 'Subjective Units of Distress', (SUDS) a rating shared by a number of therapies. The measurement is simply represented by a number from 1 - 10. The client provides the assessment of the intensity of the emotion with 10 representing the most intense and 1 the least. Emotional intensity is not something people are normally aware of so for some it can be difficult to assess accurately or even to properly identify the emotion itself, but it can be done well by most people once they become aware of the fact that they are able to.

There are many variations in the approach and application of EFT. Its founder, Gary Craig, has encouraged this with his desire to make EFT available to all and although many of the original principles still stand, the very nature of EFT promotes continual change and development. My application of EFT techniques, the descriptions of its use and the interpretation of its concepts are borne from my personal practice of EFT with real people and real issues.

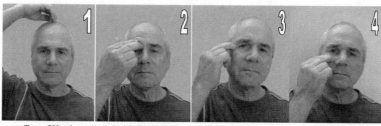

| Top of Head | Inside Eyebrow | Outside Eye | Under Eye |
| 3 Fingers | 1 or 2 Fingers | 1 or 2 Fingers | 1 or 2 Fingers |

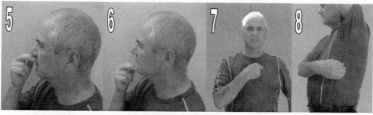

| Under Nose | Chin | Collar Bone | Side |
| 1 or 2 Fingers | 1 or 2 Fingers | 1 or 2 Fingers | 3 or 4 Fingers |

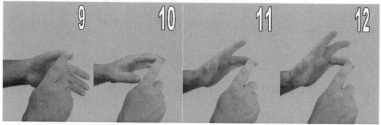

| Thumb | Index Finger | Middle Finger | Third Finger |
| 1 or 2 Fingers | 1 or 2 Fingers | 1 or 2 Fingers | 1 or 2 Fingers |

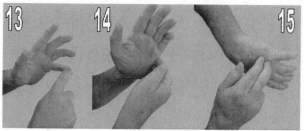

| Little Finger | Karate Chop | Gamut |
| 1 or 2 Fingers | 3 or 4 Fingers | 1 or 2 Fingers |

The procedure in detail

1) The Set-Up statement... Repeat the following affirmation three times whilst tapping on the side of the hand; the KC (Karate Chop) point:

"Even though I have this (*full and specific description of the emotion or problem*) I deeply and completely love and accept myself."

2) The tapping sequence

Tap through all the points in the set order (a minimum of seven times on each one) whilst repeating the reminder phrase each time you move to the next point. The reminder phrase is made up from a couple of words that embrace a part of the issue concisely and is usually taken from the set up statement. Its function is to maintain your focus on the problem. The more specific you can be the better will be the results. You should speak and tap at the same time.

For example:

If the problem were a phobic reaction to dogs, the 'Setup Statement' might be:

"*Even though I have this overwhelming anxiety and distress whenever I am near a dog, I deeply and completely love and accept myself.*"

The reminder phrase could be:

"*Anxiety about dogs*", or "*heart pounding when I see a dog*", or "*feeling ill and nauseous when I'm near a dog.*"

3) The 9 GAMUT protocol

Continuously tap on the Gamut point on the back of the hand whilst performing the following actions

1) Close Eyes 2) Open Eyes 3) Look hard down right (only move eyes) 4) Eyes hard down left

5) Roll eyes clockwise: 6) Roll eyes anticlockwise: 7) Hum a few notes of a tune:

8) Count to 5 9) Hum the tune again.

The 9 Gamut formed part of the original EFT procedure but most people don't routinely include this step opting to use the shortened form of EFT.

4) Repeat the tapping as above

Review or re-define the target problem and repeat the procedure if necessary adapting the 'Set-up' statement and reminder phrases to reflect any changes in the emotions or their intensity.

Quick reference guide

- Familiarize yourself with the EFT procedure above
- Choose a specific target problem (emotion, physical symptom or distressing memory) you want to work on.
- Assess the SUDS level.
- Create a "Set-up" affirmation and an appropriate reminder phrase being as specific with your language as you possibly can.
- Start tapping on the side of your hand repeating the set-up statement 3 times, and then move round all the points in sequence stating the reminder phrase at each point.
- Be persistent and continue to target and re-assess the SUDS until all aspects of the problem have cleared. Test the results thoroughly by re-visiting the initial problem and noting your response.

Experiencing the effect of EFT

The following exercise ('The Deep Breathing Exercise') is often used with groups of people and is designed to give some practice with the EFT procedure by using a non-significant aspect unlikely to touch upon emotional trauma. It is both a demonstration and a form of practice and is useful because it promotes a personal experience of a body-based change.

Before starting make sure you are familiar with the EFT procedure as detailed above.

1 Take a deep breath but don't force it, just breathe in as deeply as you can. The next step is to rate the depth of the breath it so you have something to compare against. Use a scale of 1 - 100 with 100 being lungs full to maximum capacity and 1 representing the shallowest breath you can imagine. If you are not sure just guess. Use a number that feels right.

2 Inhale deeply again and repeat the assessment. Remember that number.

3 Now begin tapping on the KC point and say the following three times to yourself out loud and with conviction.

4 *"Even though I have this constricted breathing I deeply and completely love and accept myself"*

5 Now commence tapping through the points beginning at the top of the head, repeating the reminder phrase *'my constricted breathing'* at each point.

Then tap on the Gamut point and:

1 Close your eyes

2 Open your eyes

3 Look down (without moving your head) hard left

4 Look down (without moving your head) hard right

5   Rotate your eyes clockwise

6   Rotate your eyes anticlockwise

7   Hum a few notes of a tune

8   Count from 1 - 5

9   Hum the tune again

Now tap through the points again repeating the reminder phrase.

After completing one cycle take an easy breath and relax. When you are ready, repeat the deep breath once and rate it as before.

For most people the second number will be higher than the first (Group A), for a small minority the second number will be lower than the first (Group B) and a small number of people will report no change (Group C).

Group A usually represent a significant majority. Due to the nature of the experiment it is likely that the EFT procedure was responsible for the observable change. This exercise is a simple way to demonstrate how EFT can make changes to your physical being.

Group B will be in the minority. This group will report some deterioration in their breathing ability, rating it less full that they did the first time. Often, when this happens, the tapping has stimulated underlying emotions touching upon issues that have nothing to do with their breathing yet the emergence of these 'other issues' is affecting it directly. Other feelings that surface can be tapped upon with another 'Set-up' statement and reminders. This example shows how EFT works by peeling away layer upon layer of negative emotion until the core issues are uncovered.

Group C will usually be the smallest group and one reason for this outcome may be that they may not have done the exercise properly. It is also possible that they may be so closed to the concepts of EFT that the process is being internally sabotaged.

This doesn't mean that EFT won't work for people in Group B and C but it may indicate the presence of 'Psychological Reversal' (PR). This interesting phenomenon is one of the reasons why EFT sometimes doesn't appear to work. PR is covered in depth in the Program Module 2 'Overcoming resistance'.

How does this relate to my drinking?

Drawing the focus back to alcohol, EFT, as described here can be used to uncover and collapse the negative emotions that are driving your need to drink to excess. It can also be used effectively to manage cravings in the moment. It is one of the tools in the kit but not the only one.

Consider what happens to the intensity of a craving if an expected sating is interrupted in some way. Assume that you are on your way home, really looking forward to that glass of wine when you get in. You can probably imagine just how you might feel. Everything is on track and there is every expectation that events will play out as usual. You arrive home, go indoors and put your stuff away, probably get the slippers on and make a beeline to the wine cooler – only to find you have no wine left or that the last bottle you open is corked.

For most people looking forward to something then having it denied is irritating, but in the case of a craving the reaction is often much stronger than irritation. The level of desire increases dramatically to the point of irrationality unless there is a powerful reason for that not to happen. Most people in this situation would, in all likelihood, rush out and get another bottle before doing anything else.

Cravings represent an example of emotional states that can be significantly tempered with the application of EFT. I have seen remarkable shifts in the intensity of desire in people after less than a minute of tapping. I wouldn't call it a cure, just a temporary abatement of the discomfort.

With more comprehensive use of EFT there is a more

longstanding reduction in desire often paired with an alteration to the smell of the item in question. Whether it's a drink, cigarette or a bar of chocolate, one minute it smells enticing and the next people report that the appeal has gone. Seemingly in parallel the desire to indulge just evaporates.

EFT can have a variety of other useful applications. It should not be limited just to resolving your alcohol problems but can become a helpful aid to you and those close to you whenever needed. It can be a great asset for a whole variety of different issues whether a child with a bedwetting problem, hiccups that just won't clear or a friend struggling with persistent Psoriasis.

EFT session transcript

This is part of an actual transcript of a session.

It demonstrates a guided approach where the set up statements and reminder phrases are generated by me but as far as possible reflect the client's inner world and use of language. It is a powerful way of addressing the underlying issues because I am not her and can more easily see things differently.

The transcript illustrates basic EFT skills including gentle provocation and re-framing. Much is intuitive and sometimes I go down the wrong track. A skill is to recognize when this happens and change tack accordingly. Also important is to observe for signs of emotional processing and notice when feelings shift focus.

In the transcript example, anger gives way to upset so part way through we change focus to concentrate on the upset. It is generally better to divert off and take on the emerging emotion rather than continue with the original one experienced. The newer emotion is usually more pertinent to the real issue and therefore more likely to yield better results.

The problems dealt with have a long history and are a part of the reason why this client was drinking too much. She is a successful career woman in her mid 50s who is in a long term relationship that isn't really going well. She is currently caught between working within the relationship's limitations and ending it completely. There are some good areas in this partnership such as general stability and family cohesion yet there are parts missing, or more accurately parts perceived to be missing. These feelings create distress and it is this that formed the basis of the transcribed material. It sits within the context of an overall session lasting around 90 minutes.

As the therapist I'm searching for underlying issues and, when they arise my focus is shifted toward processing of the associated negative emotions. In the conversation immediately preceding the start of the transcript it becomes clear that a memory of her husband using their children to elicit conformity or obedience from her still provokes emotion. The past events that created these feelings occurred many years ago but their effects remain alive and well in the present day. The intensity of emotion displayed confirms that they remain strong. As a therapist it is important to 'collapse' the emotions associated with past events. The following dialogue shows how EFT can be used, in a therapy context, to do that.

The discussion below is verbatim except where it wouldn't make sense in the written form such as when we both speak at the same time or when the client repeats my words whilst tapping. Where both names appear in the same box, that means that she is repeating what I'm saying almost at the same time, though slightly after. Sometimes there is a small negotiation that takes place whilst she settles on the right choice. I have added other information in brackets to convey things happening that aren't clear from the dialog alone.

The therapist is DA (me) and the client is MARY (not her real name).

DA: Even though...

MARY: Yes it does still sit there.
[She immediately interrupts referring to an intense emotion that she feels inside]

DA: MARY: Even though I feel, what was it, anger? (Yes), I still get really angry when I think of the way he used the children against me and how unfair that was on them. I deeply and profoundly love and accept myself.

DA: MARY: Even though I still feel this real anger at the way he used to use the children against me, I deeply and profoundly love and accept myself.

DA: MARY: Even though I still feel this great anger welling up inside, I deeply and profoundly love and accept myself.

[Typically the 'Set-up' phase is said three times. You will notice that I vary exactly what is said a little each time because I'm looking for feedback in her body language to indicate to me which words might have the greatest effect. The more accurate and specific the language used, the more beneficial the tapping will be.]

DA: MARY: This anger. This anger in my chest. When I think of the way he used the children against me. And how unfair that was. And that still hurts. And it still makes me angry. Despite the fact that it was years ago. And I ascribe all kinds of motivations to him. For doing this. He didn't do it on purpose. He wasn't sure. Maybe there was something else. Maybe it was just a bloke thing. Maybe it was my fault. All of these things.

[These are all 'Reminder Statements' that are said as we tap through the points, with me leading and her following. They serve to keep her mind tuned into the issue being processed. We tapped through

the sequence as we went along. She had said earlier that perhaps his actions weren't intentional or maybe he didn't realize what he was doing and she was just making a fuss so we explored this issue.]

DA: MARY: This anger. This anger. This anger. Whereas now it doesn't really matter why he did it.

DA: True?
[Still tapping]

MARY: No.
[Still tapping]

DA: It still matters does it?
[Still tapping]

MARY: I'm trying, I'm trying.
[Still tapping]

DA: It still matters to me why he did it.
[Still tapping]

MARY: It seems to.
[Still tapping]

DA: So let's put it to bed and let's say…
[Still tapping]

DA: MARY: He did this because he couldn't control me in any other way. And he thought the children were a really good tool to use and whilst that's despicable from my point of view I don't know how he felt that caused him to behave that way. This anger. Because it was wrong. It was wrong. It was wrong. It doesn't even matter why it was wrong. Do I even know what I'm talking about (*She laughs*). But I'm still angry about it. But it doesn't matter. It mattered then. It doesn't matter now. It's gone. It's in the past. He was a bit of a bastard. Fuck it, sometimes men behave that way. Fuck it, sometimes women behave that way.

[We continue tapping through the sequence whilst I remain vigilant for words and phrases that elicit a response]

DA: Take a deep breath. *[Pause]* So he had this tactic.

MARY: I'll work on that one.

DA: Is it still there? (Yes).

DA: Ok, describe to me, where is it exactly?

MARY: It's moved. It was here *[solar plexus]* and it's now up here *[upper chest and throat]*.

[The first two rounds of EFT haven't really hit the spot but the location of the feeling she first described has now shifted. This is quite a normal phenomena and it gives us a new target to work with. The next step is to focus intently and tap on that feeling. This requires that we get a more detailed description of it.]

DA: Ok, how big is it? What shape is it?

MARY: It's a long sharp thing just blocking everything there.

DA: What color is it?

MARY: Red, red.

DA: MARY: Even though I have this long sharp spike? (Yes) of red anger in my chest when I think of the way he behaved, I still deeply and profoundly love and accept myself anyway.

DA: MARY: Even though I still have this spike of red anger in my chest I deeply and profoundly love and accept myself anyway.

DA: MARY: Even though I still have this spike of red anger in my chest that I'm determined to hang onto for as long as I can, I deeply and profoundly love and accept myself.

[This is a new "Set-up" procedure for a new aspect. Initially we focused on general anger but now we have moved to exploring its physical manifestation engaging the different sensory modalities to increase effectiveness. This is typical of the layer by layer approach of EFT. Tapping on whatever emerges, be it a physical sensation, emotion, or memory will tend to lead you into the complex network of the problem.]

DA: MARY: This spike of red anger. In my chest. This long spike. When I think of it, this anger. This spike of anger. This spike of anger. This spike of anger. This spike of anger. Red and angry. Perhaps I need it. What will I do if I don't have it any more?

DA: Take a deep breath, where is it now?

MARY: It's more nebulous now, it's eased.

DA: What's the intensity?

DA: Now it's dropped from an 8 or a 9 down to a 2.

[We have a marked drop in her SUD level (Subjective Units of Distress) indicating a reduction in the intensity of the anger she was feeling. I continue with a further set up to try to eliminate it altogether.]

DA: MARY: Even though I still have some of this very justifiable remaining anger, because I just want it, I deeply and profoundly love and accept myself anyway.

DA: MARY: Even though I still have some of this remaining anger, I deeply and profoundly love and accept myself anyway.

DA: MARY: Even though I still have some of this deeply justifiable anger, I deeply and profoundly love and accept myself.

[A further series of "Set-up" statements working on the residual anger she is holding on to.]

DA: MARY: This justifiable anger. That perhaps says more about me than it does him. It's my anger. It's my anger and I'm going to keep it *[she laughs]*. And I'm not going to let anyone else have it. Because it's all mine. My self-righteous anger.

DA: Take a deep breath.

[You will notice that I stopped the sequence short on this occasion. I did this because I sensed something change and wanted to assess again at this point how she was feeling.]

DA: What's happened?

MARY: It's, it's, oh this is so boring for you. It's turned to upset now. I still get this vision in my head and I still, I can't.

The day I had to make that stand. I was forced to watch my four year old son clinging to the door handle of the car as we tried to get out and screaming in absolute abject terror "don't leave me", but I had to make the decision. I had to make that stand but it cost that child. He's never ever mentioned it since and he may not even remember it but I know it went very very deeply and that's what causes me… it's the agony.

[Her description of these events was very emotional with lots of pauses and tears. It was clear that the anger that had shielded the distress had been chipped away and the underlying vulnerability exposed.]

MARY: It's the terror he made me instill in that child. It was one of the worst moments in my life and he put us through it because he was sulking.

And that's what … that's better, that's what needed to come out.

DA: That's really good, that's good.

[She feels some relief but from my point of view we still have more work to do on the issue I sense that there are further aspects, particularly in relation to the haunting image of her son, that need exploration and processing.]

DA: No, no we are not finished yet.

DA: MARY: Even though this image of my four year old son causes me great upset, but despite that, I deeply and profoundly love and accept myself.

DA: MARY: Even though this image of my four year old son

in distress causes me great upset, I deeply and profoundly love and accept myself.

DA: MARY: Even though this image of my son causes me great upset even now, I deeply and profoundly love and accept myself.

DA: MARY: This upset. Seeing my son distressed. And crying. Because he wanted something. And he wanted me. On the other hand. I don't feel the slightest bit upset when he screamed his head off because he wanted a toy. Or he wanted to be naughty. Or he wouldn't sit at the table. Or one of the million other things he would scream his head off for. But I choose to remember this one. Because this one, I can blame me for. This upset. This upset. This upset that my son has forgotten all about. Because in his world and everybody else's world it all merges into all the other tantrums he's had. Yet I still carry it. It's my stick. Because whenever I feel worthwhile and really great I can beat myself up with it. What a fucking carry on.

[Whilst I'm going through all of these reminder statements and re-frames we are still tapping through the sequence of points and when we get to the end of a cycle we continue going round again. I stop when something changes, which in this sequence was when the humor breaks through. By the end we were both laughing at the nonsense of what she had been holding on to. When to stop, when to be provocative and when to change tack, are all guided by my intuition.]

MARY: That's good, I'm giving up ownership of it now.

DA: You are now a movie director so just create in your mind a very short movie of this scene from just before this traumatic event to just after it and when I say 'play' switch on the projector and just watch the film and stop it if you get any emotional spikes ... and 'play'.

MARY: Yes I still get it.

DA: At which point?

MARY: A small spike when I leave my husband in charge as I come out of the door and ....

DA: Stop there.

DA:MARY: Even though I feel this small spike of, what's the emotion? Anger. Even though I get this small spike of anger when I think about when I left my husband in charge, I deeply and profoundly love and accept myself.
DA: MARY: Even though I feel this small spike of anger when the film just starts and I'm leaving him in charge, I deeply and profoundly love and accept myself.

DA: MARY: Even though I feel this small spike of anger, I deeply and profoundly love and accept myself.

DA: MARY: This small spike of anger. This small spike of anger. This anger. This small spike. It's still there. Despite the fact that it was a long time ago. And everyone else has forgotten about it. I've still got it, hanging around my neck. It's always there to beat myself up with. It's always there to feel bad about. It's my anger. And nobody else's. This small spike of anger.

DA: Take a deep breath and start the film from the beginning again and ... play. Stop when you get a spike.

MARY: Not bad, I've run it through.

DA: Any spikes?

MARY: No, No.

This therapeutic interaction lasted just under 20 minutes from beginning to end. At the start there was an intense anger which during the session reduced to make way for upset. An emotionally laden memory emerges towards the end. After having run the memory, as if it were a film, whilst tapping through the points, most of the emotional distress had cleared which was evident because of the lack of any further emotional response. If she re-ran the film now there should still be no emotion attached to it. For the most part when the connection between the feelings of now and the events of the past are broken the disconnect remains.

The hurt and upset were caused by feelings of guilt, and the anger was, in part, a mechanism to limit that by channeling the blame externally. These guilty feelings served to reinforce something she already believed about herself further affecting her self-esteem. Letting it go would mean opposing some of her underlying beliefs about herself.

Her self-talk may go something like, "I know I'm not really worthy or deserving of love and my 'unfair' actions against my son just go to prove the truth of that...". You can see how someone can easily turn to alcohol as a way of managing these uncomfortable feelings.

The EFT process breaks that link and helps challenge, deconstruct and reframe these toxic beliefs. It is almost always the case that unhappiness exists alongside alcohol dependency. We tend to focus directly on the alcohol issue because it is most noticeable, the problem on the top of the pile as it were. Other problems are just seen as normal facets of life, things you just have to learn to live with. Unfortunately in the majority of cases this is just the way things are.

Flawed core beliefs are responsible for many of the negative feelings we experience. Addressing them not only reduces the need to self-medicate with alcohol but also improves self esteem along with tolerance, understanding, energy levels and motivation.

There may be other events in her life that also support the invalid core belief that, "I'm not deserving", but as has been explained not all of them need to be addressed before the belief collapses completely.

Underlying negative emotions drive our behavior although these may not themselves be evident when the behavior is being exhibited.

Reframing and the healing power of humor

Re-framing is used extensively in both EFT and Hypnosis yet often doesn't get too much of a mention. It embodies structured guidance of the client to help them see things in a different way often using humor and gentle provocation to create a shift in perspective.

One of my favorite therapeutic tools is the provocation of natural laughter. It is often accompanied by a shift in perspective that in turn can promote healing, especially if it appears at a profound moment.

Even when the gravity of the situation is severe, or the degree of trauma distressing, situations do arise that are just funny. Often when ridiculously limiting and false beliefs are exposed the humor within just explodes. Usually it's spontaneous, unexpected and initiated by the client. Every therapist has their own method of revealing an alternative perspective and the employment of humor is not uncommon. It can erupt quite by surprise and tends to have the effect of optimizing the re-frame.

Those who already use EFT will be no stranger to the comedy

that can unfold. It is a way of introducing another perspective that is so obvious it is immediately accepted.

Re-framing is the process of setting an event in a new frame of reference and viewing it from a different perspective. Perception is highly individual and how a person feels about something will always be limited by their perspective. Problems tend to be viewed from one direction only. The whole situation can be seen in quite a different light by describing it, and the emotions surrounding it, differently.

Presenting this altered perspective so that it is acceptable is the essence and skill of re-framing. Creating viable alternative options is part of the process. The quite different view that can arise challenges one's longstanding core beliefs directly, often bringing with it humor. The expression of laughter actually makes the acceptance of the revised perspective much more acceptable to the subconscious and therefore more likely to remain.

Summary

EFT is a therapy and a self-help tool and is used specifically for collapsing negative emotions. It is traditionally thought of as working on the body's bio-energetic systems but can be conceptualized in many other ways. It is still not entirely clear how it really works.

Strong negative emotions can live on long after the event or trauma that created them has passed. This is often because they, in some way, support the core belief structure. When these have been collapsed, the underlying beliefs modify as well and permanent behavioral change often results.

Humor is also a powerful way to shift an individual's perspective, particularly when combined with EFT.

Part 3 - The Program

The program you are about to start is the result of a number of years experience working with individuals with alcohol problems. It takes you through the process of stopping drinking altogether or cutting down in a step-by-step approach and allows you to move through the modules at your own pace. It requires motivation, a positive outlook and an open mind. It is not a passive process. You need to be involved and take responsibility. There is some work to do and at times it will be challenging but it will also be rewarding and enjoyable with minimal discomfort.

Work through the modules in order and try not to skip any out. They are all important. The hypnosis recordings, which can be easily downloaded from my website, should be listened to when you have read and fully understood the chapter on hypnosis and ideally after you have worked through some or all of the modules. The recordings will help you but are intended to be part of the process rather than a stand-alone solution, so use them together with the ground work and preparation, particularly the work with EFT. Remain positive and remember, if you don't have success on the first occasion see it as a blip rather than a major failure. Get your strength back, understand where you went wrong and the areas in which you need to refocus your attention and start the process again with renewed confidence.

The program will help you to change in other ways. Not only will you lessen the importance of alcohol in your life, but you will strengthen your perception of self. Firstly, however, we need to see alcohol in its true light and remove the veneer of gloss that vested interests maintain.

Chapter 8

The Program, Module 1: Analysis and understanding

If only I had known....

Information can dramatically change the way you perceive things. Sometimes these revelations crash right through everything you believed to be true in such a dramatic manner that your behavior can permanently change as a result. The whole purpose of this program is to change your relationship with alcohol so that you don't depend on it or abuse it. I hope you will realize that you have no need to fear alcohol and you will be able to drink if you wish. Fundamental changes to your perception about drinking and its place in your life can dramatically downgrade the importance of alcohol to you.

The biggest fear of them all

Drinking alcohol to excess will eventually make you sick, possibly very sick. Alcohol, when used excessively and for extended periods will cause illness to arise at some point and these alcohol-related illnesses result in the deaths of over 9,000 people each year in the UK.

From time to time there is a story arguing the health benefits of 'moderate' alcohol consumption. These are wholly unhelpful as they only serve to encourage habitual drinking. Such claims are disputed but these oppositions typically receive less attention. The alcohol industry has very deep pockets and their influence is extensive, so I'm always a bit skeptical when these 'evidence-based' studies surface.

Here are some facts you may not be aware of:

- *9,000 people die in the UK every year from alcohol-related causes*[15]
- *Annually 250,000 UK hospital admissions are alcohol-related*[16]
- *1.1 million UK adults are alcohol dependent*[17]
- *10.5 million UK adults drink above sensible limits*[18]

An alien visitor might wonder why a largely civilized society chooses a damaging, mind altering and toxic drug to underpin the social networks of business and leisure, when it is so strongly associated with aggressive behavior, road traffic accidents and death from premature illness.

There are entire populations that do not drink alcohol at all and, although we are generally under informed about these peoples and their cultures, they are in many respects, just like us. They socialize, enjoy each other's company and gather together for group events. They even watch sport on television without an alcoholic beverage in sight. The reasons why alcohol is absent from these societies isn't what really matters, it is the fact that it shows drinking alcohol to be quite unnecessary in order to enjoy a full and happy life.

Our culture, primed by the alcohol industry, encourages high consumption because it is big business. It is ruthlessly promoted resulting in an unremitting pressure to drink. People often don't connect their drinking behavior with medical problems that subsequently arise later in life, partly because it isn't widely known that alcohol causes a far greater range of illnesses than just liver disease and stomach ulcers.

There is also a significant time gap between the onset of alcohol abuse and the resultant ill health. Consider the scenario of heavy drinking starting at the age of 18 and continuing unabated through to around 40 years of age. Perhaps it is a little more measured up until the age of 60 at which point cirrhosis of the liver suddenly shows up, causing death at the age of 62. Without a clear appreciation of the association, the cause and effect are often too far apart for them to be psychologically connected. What might happen to you at 60 isn't on the radar when you are 18.

Drinkers generally prefer not to acknowledge all the links between drinking and ill health because it challenges long held beliefs about alcohol. It is all too easy to dismiss the risks of heavy drinking in favor of the supposed 'benefits of moderate drinking' referred to above.

The occasional and understated references to the less well known dangers of excessive drinking won't change the dominant drinking culture. The connection between alcohol and ill health has to be better publicized in the same way that the link between cancer, heart disease and smoking is now universally accepted.

Some medical conditions clearly associated with long term alcohol abuse are listed below[19]:

- *Cancer of the oral cavity, pharynx, esophagus and larynx*
- *Cancer of the breast, liver, colon and rectum*
- *Cirrhosis of the liver*
- *Hypertension, abnormal heart rhythms and heart failure*
- *Chronic pancreatitis*
- *Wernicke's encephalopathy, Korsakoff's syndrome, cerebellar degeneration and dementia*
- *Strokes, subarachnoid hemorrhage, tremor, hallucinations and fits*
- *Weakness, paralysis and burning sensations in the hands and feet*
- *Malnutrition and obesity*
- *Diabetes*
- *In men, loss of libido, reduced potency, shrinkage in the size of the testes and the penis and a reduction in the ability to produce sperm*
- *In women, menstrual irregularities, sexual difficulties,*

shrinkage of the breasts and external genitalia

Alcohol also interacts negatively with more than 150 medications with effects ranging from an unexpected increase in drowsiness to a risk of serious liver damage when taken with certain painkillers.

Soon after ingestion, alcohol dehydrates the body, effectively robbing it of water, thereby creating a false thirst. This doesn't tend to happen with non-alcoholic drinks. As you can see, the very notion of going for a 'drink' is a misnomer in itself. The dehydrating effect of alcohol creates a sense of needing more which in turn deprives the body of more water and so the cycle continues.

Although we speak of alcohol abuse in terms describing the individual as the 'abuser' it's actually the other way round. Alcohol abuses you more than you abuse it, and on balance it often gives more grief in the longer term than the pleasure it initially promises.

This book isn't about convincing anyone that too much alcohol causes medical problems because I suspect you already know that. Even so, I imagine that some of the conditions listed above are new to you and if listing them here helps to firm your resolve, then all well and good.

There is a plethora of information available from authorities on the medical, behavioral, relational and economic effects of heavy alcohol consumption, so I'm not about to reproduce all of them here.

This book is not about why you shouldn't drink so much, because you've probably decided that already. Its purpose is to help you make the changes you want to make on a reliable and permanent basis.

The demon drink – "Did I do that"?
People don't like to think that alcohol use is demonic in any way,

but its ability to dramatically modify behavior can create the appearance that we have been inhabited by a negative force. The disruptive and irresponsible behavior it provokes can often be quite a contrast to a more natural and sober personality.

The heavy drinker, when well established in a drinking session, typically becomes less agreeable and the person you would most like to move away from unless you are similarly intoxicated. Drunken people are generally not great company unless you are in a similar state. Behavior modified by alcohol can range from being annoying or embarrassing to extremely violent so it is no surprise that uninhibited drunken behavior often results in weeks of apology and repentance, not to mention possible criminal repercussions.

It is bizarre that we sustain such worship for concoctions that diminish normal brain function so dramatically. Drink affects your discretion and judgment, whether that is whilst driving or partying. It is a mood altering drug and often the mood you end up with is destructive in some form. The distinction between appropriate behavior and alcohol-distorted behavior can be very significant. It is well known that levels of aggression rise when alcohol is involved.

Do not underestimate the degree to which your behavior can change. Why would you want to be a hostage to this drug? Is it such a good substitute for living? Why would you want your life to be ruled by this substance? Isn't it irritating that alcohol can gain such a powerful grip on you?

The pressure to drink

There is a lot of money spent on alcohol promotion through advertising, product placement and sponsorship as well as through the influence exerted by the powerful entertainment industry.

Over £250,000,000 is spent in the UK annually on these promotional activities[20] and you have to assume they get their money's worth. There is wholehearted support by television program makers, paid or otherwise, where almost every adult program includes some form of alcohol consumption. It's worth noting that most long running UK soaps are set in and around pubs.

The British tradition of popping down to the pub is a part of the culture that is remorselessly reinforced. One has to wonder if the culture would be the same if the downsides of excessive drinking were as prominent as the 'sophisticated' drinking lifestyle.

Advertising doesn't need to be overt to be effective. A recent television drama series portrayed the leading male character drinking so much whiskey that he would be permanently unfit to drive and his female counterpart routinely sharing one and a half bottles of wine over an evening meal. Alcoholic drinks litter TV programs as a backdrop to almost every social interaction. Does this reflect society or shape it? Either way it reinforces alcohol consumption as an accompaniment to social intercourse in an unrelenting way.

Imagine a scenario where television portrayed an even balance between the upsides and downsides of drinking. Perhaps there would be more storylines involving characters who don't drink because they choose not to and not because of religious reasons or because they are 'recovering alcoholics'. Imagine that if, in popular soaps, characters suffer illnesses directly attributed to excess alcohol consumption or if they were, perhaps impotent as a result of it. Would these changes make a difference to the way we view drinking in our society?

Governments seem reluctant to ban alcohol advertising outright even though the same move made a dramatic change to the cultural perception regarding smoking. Perhaps they don't need to completely ban it but introduce a concept of equality of prominence. A system could be introduced where equal weight is given to the negative effects of alcohol whenever it is promoted.

I admit it would be quite a challenge for creative teams, but in some form the idea could have a place. Would it be acceptable to the viewer for the effects of consistently heavy consumption to damage popular TV characters? Ordinary people drink themselves to death in great numbers, so why shouldn't our 'soap stars'?

The likely effect of even a gradual change in the mass media's presentation of alcohol would be a reduction in the overall levels of consumption.

Will it happen? I suspect not, though I imagine there will be some restriction on advertising when those in power feel strong enough to take on the powerful drinks lobby. However, judging by politician's personal drinking habits, it is unlikely to come any time soon.

One of the most successful UK advertising campaigns ever run is for the stout, Guinness. In the Guinness brewery museum in Dublin, which, incidentally, is worth a visit, much is made of the astoundingly creative advertising campaigns launched over the years. Long forgotten adverts live on there and are remembered for the potent effect they have had on the levels of consumption of this world famous brand. Without such an expensive and continuous promotional effort, the brand would not be where it is today. Don't underestimate the power of this constant and unremitting persuasion.

As a result of this insidious pressure we have come to accept things that are not really true as being undisputable facts – such as the association between food and wine, drinking and having fun or drinking pints of beer and manliness. The use of alcohol is so entrenched in our culture that to take a different personal view about it (even though it would be more honest and accurate) could create considerable tension within one's existing social relationships. If and when you decide to change your drinking habits, these relationship challenges will have to be considered.

Think about events you attend or have attended in the past that are alcohol-dominated. How about those friends where the only thing you have in common is that you drink too much together? Consider for a moment how odd is the concept of choosing to 'get completely pissed'? Why would one want to relinquish control, become ill or behave badly and dangerously, all at considerable expense? Yet I have done this too many times to remember all of them and perhaps you have too. We must not forget that alcohol is a drug like any other except that it is legal and, perhaps because of the tax revenues it generates, is also positively encouraged.

As your relationship with alcohol changes, other material things will also change. You will have more time on your hands and more money in your pocket, some health issues will just disappear and you may even lose a little weight. You may also find that some of your relationships have so little binding them together that they might end. Others will undoubtedly strengthen. You need to be prepared for this and allow it to happen.

In time you will see the comedy in the way you used to behave and you will become aware of your life opening up and diversifying. Old friendships that were based solely on drinking may end and you will begin to notice all the people who don't drink, the people who you never even knew existed.

We live in a society that regards the consumption of alcohol as highly desirable. In some work-hard play-hard office cultures heavy drinking behavior is often a necessary qualification to belong to the team and keep your job. Because alcohol has become such a significant part of our culture and a routine part of everyday life, its destructiveness is often overlooked and scarcely questioned.

This acceptance of alcohol becomes part of your 'writing on the wall'. This EFT concept is useful as it challenges our understanding of that which is 'true' and that which isn't. The 'writing' contains messages, rules and beliefs that we unquestioningly accept as fact. Much of the content would have been written by parents, relatives, school teachers, peers, friends and some would have developed as a result of difficult life experiences. But because such a lot was provided by others early in life, much of what is on your wall is probably incorrect. Wrong or right, these 'writings' have a fundamental role in how we behave and how we feel.

Alcohol and its effect on relationships

Most relationships come under pressure when an unhealthy use of alcohol is involved. We interact with other people in our lives in a range of different ways. We rarely analyze what influences those relationships and we can often misjudge the effect of our behavior on these connections. If we were to conduct an analysis of our relationships, it might provide a platform to make conscious decisions about the changes that are needed. We can work to improve the relationships we are determined to keep and identify those we might want to allow to lapse.

This process might help us to act more in line with our desires and give us more control. It's much easier to manage or repair relationships when you understand how your behavior impacts them.

Personal wellbeing is markedly influenced by interactions with others so it makes sense to understand the nature of these, what binds them and how to modify our behavior to improve them. Individual and group relationships are all affected in some way by drinking. Some will be strengthened by it and others will be damaged. What's important is that we have some control over what happens.

Each individual in a relationship, be it husband or wife, boyfriend or girlfriend, parent or child, has certain needs and expectations that can either be met by the other party or by an external activity.

Ideally, these external activities are healthy and positive and are a strengthening factor rather than a damaging one. The problem with alcohol abuse is that it is inherently toxic to relationships. In addition, it is often just one party that has the issue with alcohol, with the other one suffering markedly because of it.

One can consider a personal relationship as a series of connecting strands between two people. I call these connecting strands 'relationship channels'. Each end of the channel represents the emotional need of the individual with respect to this aspect of their relationship. These emotional needs can be called 'channel-end needs' and it may help to think of them as ranging in intensity between 0 and 10. The chart below is one way of conceptualizing relationships better. It can help you to represent and determine what must change to restore harmony.

For some relationships, harmony between the parties depends upon the needs matching or being similar. For others, balance is best represented when they are apart. Individuals in relationships still need personal space and activities that provide this fall within the allowable parameters of the relationship. The relationship can positively flourish even when some needs seem far apart. For example, consider a husband and wife relationship where the husband likes fishing and the wife has no interest. This kind of activity can provide the space both parties need and in that context can reflect strength rather than weakness. It represents an emotional need being met for both, in this case *personal space*, so whilst the activities occupying them are different the needs being met are in line.

Stress almost always occurs if a disparity exists between each party's individual needs when they should be aligned. In these instances the wider the gap, the greater the stress. When a threshold is reached something has to give and that can often result in the complete breakdown of the relationship.

The relationship chart shows a number of relationship

Relationship Channels and End Channel Needs

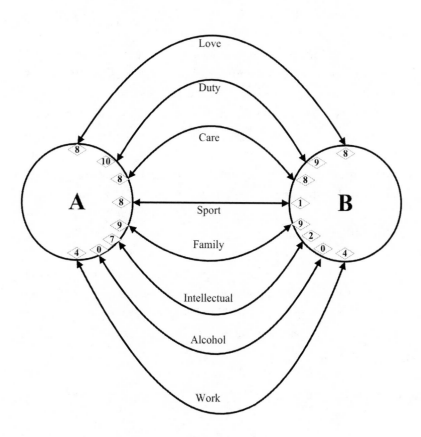

channels, some of which have similar channel-end needs and others that do not. Your chart may be different and may have more or fewer channels depending on your circumstances. See it as a way of looking at the interactions between the people in your life to create a better understanding.

This process helps you identify areas of your life that might need attention. It isn't necessary to identify every relationship channel that exists with every person in your life but it is important to include those you see as more important. If your partner also drinks heavily and the relationship is stable you may want to examine other important personal relationships with parents or children, siblings or friends. At least one of these is likely to be in difficulty as a result of your drinking, if not all of them. It is important to be completely honest with yourself.

When completing the exercise, it's better if the intensity of the channel-end need is assessed both by you and the other person. If it isn't possible or appropriate to do this openly by showing them the chart, then you should fill in the numbers yourself, ideally following an informal discussion. It isn't possible to accurately assess how others might feel about such things without some communication with them either directly or otherwise.

Many people who seek my help to overcome alcohol addiction do so because their relationship is under threat and not because they are physically ill or socially destitute. In many cases there is a lack of explicit acknowledgement that a problem exists. More frequently one partner is unaware or dismissive of it. Often the substance abuse is concealed and the other is unaware of the extent of the problem and may even be under the impression that it has been resolved. If you are secretly drinking and your relationships are showing signs of strain then it may well be time to act.

When considering channel-end needs, think about the constancy of that need and whether or not it could be met elsewhere. A need to indulge in sport, for example, occurs periodically, while the need to be loved or consulted or the need for honesty is constant. With some channel end needs, e.g. monogamy, the need is ever present and there is no possible satisfaction elsewhere.

A common problem with the alcohol channel is the altered behavior of the intoxicated partner. It directly affects the fabric of the interaction. The personality changes that occur through intoxication typically heighten distress for the other party in the relationship. It is under these conditions that stress develops and changes need to take place to redress the balance.

There is invariably some social discomfort that occurs when drinking habits are changing. A typical feeling expressed by someone who is trying to stop drinking as much, but who is still connected to a group that drinks heavily, is a sense of isolation or even exclusion. "They all get pissed and I can't". This generates a range of difficult feelings because longstanding friendships are involved and to break a habit, to be the odd one out, to be the 'non-drinker', creates emotional tension. It's important to understand which ones are true friendships by looking at the relationship channels and their respective needs.

If a friend is a true friend then they ought to meet you halfway, be flexible and understanding and show compromise. If they are just an acquaintance or if the only relationship channel that exists between you is solely the alcohol then you should really question whether or not you need them in your life at all.

Maybe the boys' or girls' night out in a bar might change in some way. Perhaps you might introduce other ideas for social time, such as meeting for a coffee or going to the gym or the cinema, activities that eliminate the drinking whilst maintaining the friendship.

In short, strengthen the relationships that are worth saving and let go of the ones that aren't.

Altered behavior brought on by alcohol may distort channel

end needs that are stable and functional when sober.

An example is the effect of alcohol on sexual desire and performance. At the extreme alcohol can result in complete abstinence or infidelity. In the case of the latter, such behavior is usually excused as 'innocent flirting' but for the sober partner such protestations do not prevent the feelings of hurt and betrayal. Empathy is an emotion severely suppressed by alcohol. Sometimes the stress and anger provoked is so acute that long periods of silence and even separate bedrooms can ensue.

Use the chart to analyze your relationships and assess the effect that alcohol may be having on them. If you feel able, show the chart to your partner so that you can both work on it. You will need to address the problems at some point because in all likelihood the difficulties manifesting now will only increase if the drinking behavior continues unchanged.

Summary

Formal analysis of a situation with accurate information to hand can, in itself, change how you feel about something sufficiently to prompt a behavioral shift. It could be just that one fact you didn't know about that completely overhauls the way you perceive an issue and, in turn, increases your motivation to change.

Understanding how alcohol affects the body and the risks you are taking with your health as well as the subtle but powerful social influences that keep the problem alive are important factors in this stage of the program.

Of fundamental importance is an appreciation of how relationships are affected by drink. Understanding the different expectations and needs at play can be a strong motivator to change behavior.

Chapter 9

The Program, Module 2: Overcoming resistance

Conceptualizing 'Psychological Reversal'

Some people experience dramatic change with therapy and others don't seem to respond at all or their response is limited. On occasions and for no obvious reason progress is slower and results are harder to come by. Some people have to wait longer and work harder and some haven't yet found the approach that really works for them or they just give up too easily. Some just start to make headway in their journey and then they do something to disadvantage themselves and the process.

So why do therapy interventions work well for some and not others? Why do these blocks to healing exist? What drives this seemingly in-built mechanism to self-sabotage?

There are, of course, lots of possible explanations but it is certainly worth considering factors that will inhibit progress including internal resistance driven by subconscious fears. This idea is described in EFT and TFT circles as 'Psychological Reversal' (PR), and it is considered the most common imped- iment to recovery. It can present in various forms and is also thought to account for mistakes in word, letter or number order, confusing of left and right and generally saying or doing the opposite of what you intend. When subconscious self sabotage obstructs progress it tends to do that whatever form of thera- peutic interventions are employed.

We have learnt that problems can be conceptualized as disruptions to the flow of energy through the body, this being the central idea in Traditional Chinese Medicine. Some understand 'Psychological Reversal' itself to be a disruption or distortion to the body's energy flow or orientation, perhaps even a polarity shift in the system. It is claimed that energy flow, including polarity shifts can be objectively demonstrated using standard electrical measurement devices such as voltmeters and ammeters, not to mention proprietary and complicated ones such as 'biographs'. It may be, of course, that complex and impressive machinery has more to do with the marketing of the therapy than the definitive measurement of energy.

Many, however, conceptualize 'Psychological Reversal' simply as an unconscious defense mechanism, rooted in a rational fear. It can be seen to encompass those hidden reasons to resist change, as a result of common anxieties associated with the change. Some have pointed to physical causes or 'toxins' that may include certain types of food, clothing or other elements in the immediate environment. It is possible that these toxins are having an effect on the body's energy system, if in fact one truly exists, in the same way that an allergen can create a visible allergic reaction in the body. Such toxins, whilst not considered true allergens in the medical sense, are held to exert their influence 'energetically' in a way that we don't fully understand.

Or perhaps the perceived effect of toxins can also be explained psychologically i.e. an effect exerted due to subconscious associations with the environment you are in or the clothes you are wearing.

'Psychological Reversal', whatever its underpinnings, can obstruct the ability of an individual to make changes and heal regardless of the external intervention applied.

In both EFT and TFT, there are techniques for correcting the 'reversal', something that can be done in seconds. In my view, these blocks or fears represent the most significant obstruction to EFT, in fact to all therapeutic approaches.

Hidden benefits
People have to want to change before it can happen. A form of

'reversal' that often exists is when a person consciously wants to change but on a subconscious level they have deep reservations. This inner conflict is complex and quite often people cannot reconcile it alone. This book aims to support this reconciliation process.

As well as being a body-based processing technique, EFT also embodies a counseling component which is an integral part of all talking therapies. The employment of more traditional cognitive counseling strategies plays an important role in reframing one's perspective to identify subconscious obstruction.

To illustrate the issue let's consider a female client, Rachael, who struggles to control her eating and is clinically obese. She's 30 years old, intelligent and pretty, 5' 6" in height and weighs 400 pounds (that's about 28 stone). She has a desperate desire to lose weight enhanced now by the recent emergence of joint pain making it difficult for her to walk. The problems with her joints are directly associated with her extreme size.

You might think that here is a person who has all the reasons in the world to do something about her weight and on a conscious level she will agree with you. However, despite therapy nothing changes. The weight remains the same despite her declared intent to lose it. There seems to be a strong suggestion of 'Psychological Reversal' at play and it seems to be stopping her from making any kind of progress.

In this scenario let's assume medical tests have shown that the obesity isn't due to any glandular or other underlying identifiable medical condition. The obesity is driven and sustained by excessive intake, with a significant proportion of high calorie, low nutrient, junk food and/or alcohol. To maintain such extreme weight the consumption levels have to be extraordinary, so it follows that if, as we assume, emotions are driving the behavior, they are very powerful indeed.

In her day to day life people have to adapt to accommodate her. She cannot stand for long so when she goes to the pub with friends a space has to be cleared for her to sit. Traveling is also quite complicated and special measures have to be taken to accommodate her on public transport. Because she is so large almost every activity requires some degree of modification or support by others so that she can participate. This is a person for whom it is impossible to move around and function anonymously.

When trying to identify what may lie behind the 'Psychological Reversal' one has always to ask "What are the downsides of change?", "What is so important that it is keeping the problem alive?"

We can see that there may be some (albeit dysfunctional) benefits of being so big. She is always noticed, often the centre of attention and people go out of their way to do things for her. There is no space for her to be alone or insignificant. Were she to lose weight she may no longer warrant these special considerations. Without the attention she may feel lonely and worthless, reinforcing negative core beliefs about her self-worth. It may be that the fear of this alternate reality, the dramatic change in attention that would ensue is inhibiting change. In a peculiar way her subconscious places greater value on the 'benefits' of her size than it does on the damage that the weight is causing.

This is not a rational judgment because the subconscious doesn't 'think' rationally. Severe consequences such as serious illness or the prospect of an early death may be less important in the realms of the subconscious mind than the benefits of maintaining the destructive behavior. The underlying emotional drivers can be incredibly powerful which is why people continue their chosen path of self-destruction despite consciously acknowledging the harm being caused.

The 'hidden benefits' of maintaining destructive behaviors are almost always centered on low self esteem. You should be aware that there is constant subconscious analysis of the value of the status quo against the downsides of change. Addressing that is often critical in smoothing the path to real change. Identifying and processing the associated emotions can unearth the invalid beliefs upon which these perceived benefits are based.

The issue of extreme obesity can also stem from a subconscious desire to be sexually unattractive. This specific connection is well documented and is an attempt to deflect unwanted sexual attention, perhaps driven by long past distressing sexual experiences.

Similar potential upsides exist for alcohol misuse issues despite the collateral damage that may be taking place. All of your heartfelt desire and conscious determination to drink less will almost certainly be frustrated in some way by the downsides of change. If subconsciously you believe these changes would impact your life in a negative way then your efforts will be hampered unless the potential reversals are addressed.

If your subconscious doesn't want you to change, it will usually win.

Fear of outcomes

Hidden benefits of maintaining the status quo forms one part of 'Psychological Reversal'. Others tend to be based on fear and they come in various shades. By way of example, let's consider a client with a relationship problem. Anna wants her relationship with her husband to improve and she wants to be happy, but she can't help but feel it is going nowhere. This affects her motivation and zest for life. She's gone off sex but feels compelled to indulge to keep her husband happy. She wants to work but can't find a decent job and she is rarely interested in going out. She also feels the need to drink a few glasses of wine every evening to relax and get away from it all.

Anna has been struggling for some time with her husband because of a variety of issues mostly revolving around his aggressive behavior. Yet she argues that she loves him very much and cannot bear the thought of them separating. She perceives herself as the 'glue' holding them together and thinks that if only she were a better partner then everything would be fine. In therapy, she explains away his unacceptable behavior by taking the blame herself.

The thought of the relationship ending creates a strong negative emotional response in her. As she cannot entertain the possibility of breaking up, she searches for ways to cope and uses rationalizations to tolerate it. One clear option open to her is to end the relationship but as that option is not being entertained in any way it will retain a 'charge' and may actually propagate the reversal. Other specific worries that may be contributing to her subconscious resistance include "What will happen to the children?", "What will I live on?", "Where will I live?", "How will I cope alone?"

Her perspective is undoubtedly colored by powerful fears about herself, her life and her future. These fears act as an obstacle to meaningful change. Until the range of outcomes can be considered, contemplated, talked about and even visualized without generating the same level of emotion, the unknown will stand as an obstruction to her achieving wellbeing.

It is the internal emotional and physical turbulence driving her distress, not the actuality of events, be they in the past, the present, or potentially in the future. It is not what has happened or what might happen that is important, but how she feels when she thinks about it.

Reducing the emotional response one has to the possibility of 'bad' outcomes often has to happen before progress can be achieved. Whilst this reversal is in place, the system will be under stress with consequent effects on behavior. Ironically the stress Anna is under because of repressed emotions is actually contributing to the relationship problem.

EFT is a particularly effective tool for collapsing negative emotions as well as having specific built-in mechanisms for countering 'Psychological Reversal'.

For those with alcohol problems it may be the fear that you will never be 'cured', that the temptation to drink will always exist, that for the rest of your life you will continually need to adopt management strategies to prevent you relapsing and destroying everything. It is not the 'reality' of these outcomes that is of prime importance but how you feel about them potentially happening. Counter intuitively, you may need to first accept that you will never get over your dysfunctional relationship with alcohol for it to change.

To succeed you have to 'emotionally' understand and accept that you may also fail.

It is likely that buying this book isn't your first attempt to try and change your drinking habits. For some it may be the most recent in a series of attempts to give up or cut down. This can lead to an increasing sense of hopelessness and fear of ultimate failure. A fear of outcomes is the subconscious's way of preparing for failure. Again, it isn't what the outcome might be, or its degree of difficulty that is the problem, it is how you feel about it.

Consider what your subconscious might be saying regarding your plans to cut down or stop drinking:

- *"You can't do this, you've tried before"*.
- *"It's too difficult, almost everyone fails."*
- *"The relapse rate is high."*
- *"You're not strong enough, you always fail."*
- *"Face it you're stuck with this problem for life."*

Throughout your life every failure you have experienced is playing a role here. Just when you could do with support and direction, your subconscious mind reminds you about all your weaknesses and failures.

So what happens then?

You tend to mitigate the probability of yet another failure by making an excuse, explaining why it is unlikely to work or why now is not the right time. It then becomes easier to fail or to accept defeat, because it isn't really your fault.

The excuses we make are many and varied but here are some examples:

- *"I have an addictive personality."*
- *"The therapy wasn't working anyway."*
- *"I couldn't afford the sessions."*
- *"I was ill and couldn't attend. Now I've lost the momentum."*
- *"I'll do it when I'm 20, 30, 40, 50, etc."*
- *"I don't really drink that much anyway."*
- *"What's the point, I read an article that said red wine was good for you."*
- *"There's too much going on at the moment, it's not a good time."*

A man walks into a bar and after a while begins chatting to another man. The conversation drifts on to the London Marathon. The first man says "I did it this year for the first time and although it was difficult I might have a go again next year". The other man says "I would love to do it but I can't now because I've got this wooden leg" as he taps lightly with his knuckles just below the knee to emphasize and validate the fact. In reality, the degree to which even such an obvious disability such as this would prevent him from doing things is questionable and not a clear fact. To some it would be enough to stop them walking more than a few yards. Others might play football or compete in athletic events such as the Paralympics.

I remember the story that broke just before the 2008 Olympic Games when Oscar Pistorious, an athlete whose legs had both been amputated below the knee, wanted to enter the 400 meters race using carbon-fiber prostheses designed for sprinting. The use of the legs was banned by the International Association of Athletics Federations on the grounds that they gave the user *an advantage*, a ruling that was subsequently overruled by the Court of Arbitration for Sport with some innovative and convoluted rationale.

In essence, they argued that it was fine to use the legs as long as he didn't win the race.

What comes through strikingly clearly though is Oscar Pistorious's perception of his disability and his determination for it not to prevent him from achieving his desires.

Beware of your excuses. They may not be as obvious or compelling as an amputation but they may still be there. Challenge them and be honest with yourself.

It is also common to experience anxiety with respect to potential success, or in a competitive environment, a *fear of winning*. These feelings are generated at the subconscious level and often exert a detrimental effect on performance despite an overtly conscious desire to do well.

Many of us will have experienced the effect of these feelings directly. If you have ever been called upon to give a presentation you will know exactly what I mean. Even if the audience is inherently friendly, less experienced presenters will experience physical symptoms including a fluttery stomach, dryness around the lips and an inexplicable inability to pronounce words properly.

Imagine the professional golfer, tennis player or boxer. What separates them from the amateur is the ability to overcome their subconscious fears and limit the effect they have on their performance. It's often said that, when a less experienced but talented sportsperson fails just when it seemed victory was assured, it was because of the fear of success. It seems more rational to have a fear of losing rather than winning yet it sometimes feels better to the subconscious to lose – at least you were in control. It is a well known phenomenon, often referred to as 'self sabotage', and it can manifest in most stressful and competitive situations including exams, interviews and sporting competitions.

Imagine for a moment what your subconscious might be thinking during a competitive game:

- *"You can't win; you're too young / inexperienced."*
- *"How dare you beat him, he is the best! How can you possibly beat the best?"*
- *"You're so lucky to even get this far."*
- *"You are not good enough yet, wait until next time."*

Addressing resistance or 'Psychological Reversal'

We have seen that simply facing up to the possible outcomes and emotionally engaging with the potential implications is sometimes enough in itself to overcome resistance. Also, being honest with yourself about the potential hidden benefits of holding on to a problem can be hugely enlightening. What to do though if this doesn't do the trick? What if the resistance feels like it is at a deeper level?

EFT talks a lot about this issue and argues that the most effective ways of overcoming or reversing 'Psychological Reversal' include:

- Repeating affirmations of self acceptance (which explains the reason for the statement "…….I completely accept myself", which forms part of the standard EFT set up)

- The action of tapping repeatedly on the side of the hand closest to the little finger, referred to as the 'Karate Chop Point', or rubbing a specific point on the upper chest, just above the breast and below the collar bone on the left side, referred to as the 'Sore Spot'

Note: The sore spot isn't included in the pictures of the tapping points because it is rarely used nowadays. It hurts when you press it with finger tips, so it is quite easy to locate. You only need to consider using this spot if tapping on the KC point isn't working for you. Rub it firmly with two fingers in a circular motion.

I would advise making the resistance to change a target for the EFT in its own right. This may be necessary before any shifts will occur. In essence, focus on the fear of addressing the addiction before working on the addiction itself.

Re-read the chapter on EFT and make sure you are comfortable using this technique. Further insights regarding how to approach this issue of resistance and other foci for the EFT are provided in the next module so it is probably worth reviewing this first. You will soon understand how to tackle this issue. It may help to practice using the EFT on other issues, perhaps not related in any way to the alcohol problem. You will see for yourself how it works to reduce resistance both consciously and subconsciously.

Finally, I want to briefly consider the subject of your environment and in particular, the issue of toxins. Some advise screening your environment for possible toxins, in the food you eat, the clothes you wear and the toiletries you use. Taken to the extreme this may even include the people you spend time with. If a toxin is suspected, it could be excluded for a trial period.

Identifying and eliminating toxins isn't something I've found necessary very often and I'm not entirely convinced about the degree to which they can disrupt therapy. However, that said, I do believe that environmental factors are important and do have an impact. If something just feels wrong, even if it is something you are fond of superficially, it does no harm to exclude it from your life and see if it makes a difference. Sometimes making a change to your external world helps facilitate internal change.

Summary
There are a range of emotional states and cognitive traps that obstruct or inhibit your ability to make permanent changes. They

are often supported by your fundamental beliefs about yourself. In EFT terms this resistance is known as 'Psychological Reversal'. It can take many forms but most are rooted in fear.

Progress is much more achievable when the hidden obstructions are made conscious and challenged directly.

EFT is particularly effective at collapsing negative emotional connections and limiting beliefs. It also has specific techniques for countering 'Psychological Reversal'.

Chapter 10

The Program, Module 3: Resolving issues

The idea is to develop an understanding of how you might start to identify and target, using EFT, the specific emotions, needs, fears, blocks, limiting beliefs, memories and triggers that are relevant to you and your drinking behavior.

If you go to an experienced therapist they will help you elicit this information but, for the most part, it is possible to do it yourself, unless of course you feel you need the external support.

Emotional states

The specific emotions that we feel can be easily deciphered with a bit of practice. Below, I have included a list of common negative emotional states. It is, of course, not exhaustive. Notice how you feel when you read them out loud. Familiarize yourself with the list and practice trying to match how you are feeling with the named emotion. Circle the ones that resonate. You can add or remove words if you wish so that it works for you. What is most important is that you are able to find a word that matches how you are feeling.

Towards the end of this module, you will start to realize that the language you use, together with the tapping, is fundamentally important.

- *Fear*
- *Anger*
- *Guilt*
- *Pride*
- *Sadness*
- *Resentment*

- *Jealousy*
- *Anxiety*
- *Frustration*
- *Regret*
- *Loneliness*
- *Grief*
- *Self-Pity*
- *Depression*
- *Shame*
- *Denial*
- *Worry*

Needs that drinking satisfy

As we discussed earlier in the book, people drink alcohol for a reason. It serves a function. It meets a need. It is critical to identify these in order to understand and deconstruct them. A good way to uncover the functions that alcohol serves for you is to:

- Think of the drink-related **activities** you do on a regular basis
- Then consider the **needs** that you might be satisfying by drinking alcohol when you do these activities

I have included an example list below. Try the exercise for yourself, it can be eye opening.

Activity: **Going out with friends**

Reasons to drink (i.e. needs being met):
- *To chill out and relax*
- *To feel part of the group and meet shared expectations*
- *To celebrate (birthdays, promotions)*
- *To feel like I'm letting my hair down*

- *To get drunk and forget*
- *To manage my social anxiety*

Activity: **Going to a restaurant**
- *To comply with social etiquette (e.g. having wine with a meal)*
- *To not stand out*
- *To look sophisticated*
- *To manage my anxiety around food*

Activity: **Watching TV alone**
- *To unwind or switch off after a stressful day*
- *To counter a feeling of loneliness*
- *To indulge ('me' time)*

Activity: **Watching sports with friends**
- *To fit the cultural stereotype*
- *To meet the expectations of the group*
- *To manage social anxiety*
- *To cope with the excitement of the game*

Activity: **Going on a girls' night out**
- *To belong*
- *To not stand out*
- *To meet the group expectation*
- *To celebrate*
- *To rebel*

Activity: **Drinking at home alone**
- *To stop the lonely feeling*
- *To blur how terrible I feel about myself*
- *To pass the time*
- *To help me sleep*
- *To enjoy my own company*

You can see that most of the needs listed fall into one of the following three categories:

- Meeting social expectations
- Belonging
- Anaesthetizing

Common fears, blocks and reversals

As we have seen in the previous chapter, barriers often stand in the way of positive change. They are usually a result of a fear of some eventuality. Here are some of the more common ones. Mark the ones that relate to you. Adapt them as you see fit.

- *Fear of never getting over the problem*
- *Fear of getting over the problem – expectations, responsibilities*
- *Fear of exhausting all the options*
- *Fear of the withdrawal symptoms*
- *Fear that it's not safe to stop drinking*
- *Fear that it will negatively affect others if I stop drinking*
- *Fear of feeling deprived*
- *Fear of no longer having an excuse*
- *Fear of being sober / bored*
- *Fear of seeing the true / real me*
- *Fear I won't be liked / fun*
- *Feeling that I don't deserve to be free*

Common limiting beliefs

We have established that beliefs are based on individual perception and they are not always right or helpful. They can also limit your trust in yourself and your potential. It is essential to address these beliefs before trying to stop drinking or cut down. It will make the whole process a lot easier. See if you connect with any of these. They are some of the more common beliefs that people struggle with in this area:

- *I don't really think I can ever stop drinking*
- *I don't trust myself to survive without alcohol*
- *I've tried this before and it didn't work*
- *I'm just going through the motions because I know I can't really stop*
- *I don't think I can really change*
- *I still won't be happy even if I stop*
- *I can't just give up this need*
- *It's in my genes*
- *Once an alcoholic, always an alcoholic*
- *Even if I stop I know it will only be temporary*
- *I know of so many others who have also failed*
- *I can't imagine life without alcohol*
- *I need a drink to relax*
- *I'm a drinker and no one can tell me otherwise*

Common triggers

Alcohol-related cues can be powerful things. The subconscious forms associations with normal everyday experiences or stimuli that can become triggers for a relapse. It's better to predict these and deal with them up front. Here are some of the more common ones:

- *Feeling lonely*
- *Feeling worthless*
- *Feeling bored/restless*
- *Feeling hopeless*
- *Feeling excited*
- *Feeling inhibited*
- *Feeling overwhelmed*
- *Certain foods*
- *Seeing someone drink on TV / in real life*
- *The smell of alcohol*
- *Off-licenses / Bars*

- *The end of the working day*
- *Weekends*
- *Nights out*
- *Watching sport*
- *Summertime*
- *Christmas*
- *Birthdays*
- *Being with friends who are drinking*
- *Using drugs*

Difficult memories

Traumatic memories can be distressing but if they remain unprocessed, they can significantly affect how you feel. Emotions can often get locked away and engaging them is an important step towards resolving your issues with alcohol. If you find that processing them becomes overly upsetting try working with a skilled therapist who can help you find a way to deal with these issues in a more comfortable manner. When dealing with significant traumas, including any form of abuse, you may initially want to seek some advice and direction.

I have included this exercise primarily to get you thinking. In the space below or on a separate piece of paper, make a list of the 5 most difficult memories that you have. Try to identify those with the most 'charge' associated with them - those that you know from experience provoke the strongest response emotionally and physically. As you write the list ensure that you do not allow yourself to get absorbed by the memories. Remain objective. Only engage the memory properly when you are ready to do some processing work.

1.

2.

3.

4.

5.

Working with your lists

Once pen has been put to paper issues become much more difficult to ignore and there is a greater incentive to act. Before considering how you can use your lists to move you forward in this process of change, it's worth re-visiting the EFT chapter, in particular the transcript at the end.

The way to begin is to draw out particular words or statements relevant to you and your problem. You can use the above lists and select those that particularly resonate with you, or add other ones not listed above. Work through the different categories systematically.

Integrate the words you choose into the standard EFT set-up statement:

"Even though I have this.......................I completely accept myself".

Examples from each category are shown below:

Emotions:
"Even though I feel this *immense guilt* about my drinking, I completely accept myself"

Needs:
"Even though I use alcohol *to manage my loneliness* and I'm not sure what I will do without it, I completely accept myself"

Fears /Blocks:

"Even though I'm scared that if I stop drinking *people will see the real me and maybe they won't like me*, I completely accept myself"

Limiting beliefs:

"Even though I'm convinced *I will fail as I have failed so many times before*, I completely accept myself"

Triggers:

Even though I'm scared I'm going to miss that drink *when I get home from work* and I don't think I can do this, I completely accept myself

Memories:

Even though I have this memory of…………………………….. ,
I completely accept myself"

Once you have decided upon a few statements (about 10-15), it helps to rate them according to how much you relate to them when you read them. Say them out loud or get someone else to read them to you.

Decide on the level of emotional 'charge' they hold. Assess each one and give it a number between 1 and 10 according to how much it resonates with you when you hear it. 10, represents a very significant reaction and 1, represents no reaction at all.

Separate off statements that score highly and think of appropriate reminder phrases to be used as you tap round the points. Once you have your statement and the reminder phrase, you are set to go with the tapping.

Say the 'Set-up' statement three times whilst tapping on the side of your hand, then work through each point in turn, tapping about 8-10 times whilst repeating the reminder phrase.

Check your emotional response to the statement after a couple of rounds and proceed accordingly. Either continue with further rounds of tapping until the emotional response drops completely, or create new 'Set-Up' statements and reminder phrases to reflect any emergent thoughts, memories, emotions or physical sensations.

You may find that new, seemingly unrelated material just comes to mind creating further avenues for you to explore. As you become more confident try and become creative with the technique. Change things a little here and there and see the effect.

Other useful lists

Pros and Cons of stopping (or cutting down)

There are always gains and losses with every decision or choice. Sometimes it helps to make a list of them. It gets your mind working and focuses your attention on the issues. If it feels like it would be a useful exercise, take the time to have a think about it properly.

PROS (OF STOPPING)

-
-
-
-
-

CONS (OF STOPPING)

-
-
-
-
-

Benefits and downsides of alcohol

BENEFITS (OF ALCOHOL)

-

-

-

-

-

DOWNSIDES (OF ALCOHOL)

-

-

-

-

-

Ways I intend to occupy my time when I stop / cut down

Whether you like it or not, you are going to have a lot more time on your hands when you stop or cut down your drinking. You will also have much more energy and drive. It's worth taking a moment to consider what you might like to do with this time. Think of a few realistic ideas:

1.

2.

3.

4.

5.

Try to involve others in your list making. You will, by definition, see things from your own perspective but contribution from others, particularly those who know you well, will almost certainly add new dimensions that will expand your under-standing of your own issues. You may well see things in a way that you may not have done before.

Your life and all the things you believe about it have your individual frame of reference and it is likely that somewhere within that perspective lies the cause of your distress.

Summary

It is important to start somewhere in your quest to understand and modify your drinking behavior. This chapter aims to give you some direction and focus. Lists are a great way to kick-start this process but it helps to work with someone else if you feel able. Try to use your intuition as much as possible to guide this process.

It is helpful to translate these personal insights into 'Set-Up' statements and use EFT (tapping) to process the negative emotions and collapse unhelpful beliefs that underpin your unwanted behavior.

Seeing things from another perspective is always helpful and often essential.

Ongoing development

The forerunner to this book is my on-line interactive program that you can find at:

www.control-your-drinking.co.uk.

The web site incorporates an interactive program where subscribers receive regular emails at predetermined intervals providing guidance through a structured program to help them change their relationship with alcohol. Included, as a part of the program, are the two hypnosis CD's, currently available, (Alcohol Control 1 and Alcohol Control II).

From the website came this book, which includes much more detail than can easily be presented on a screen. It grew as a necessary development of the on-line program started in 2007, whereas from this publication the on-line program will effectively become an extension of the book.

The benefits of a website are that it can be easily and regularly updated and can include additional material such as audio downloads. The content of the website is constantly developing.

There are opportunities for people to communicate with each other through forums as well as a help section where advice can be sought. It is an interactive space to support ongoing change.

Chapter 11

The Spiritual connection

What is spirituality?

It is said that Carl Jung recommended spirituality as a cure for alcoholism for a patient of his, one Rowland Hazard III. Being hopelessly addicted and beyond help by Jung's psychoanalytical techniques Jung postulated that only a life changing spiritual experience would be able to undo Hazard's addiction to alcohol.[21]

This led Hazard to join the Oxford Group, a spiritually based group for personal change, and it seems that he achieved a period of extended sobriety as a result. However, his ongoing struggle with alcoholism ultimately led to the formation of Alcoholics Anonymous, though it seems he was never actually a member of the organization.

Acknowledging spirituality changes lives. When such a transformation happens to a person, it can overwrite a lifetime of negativity overnight. Spiritual awareness not only allows you to alter the level of importance that alcohol has in your life but it may also change your entire perspective on the value of your own existence.

I've discussed changing beliefs by subconscious suggestion and using methodologies such as EFT (something that Jung did not have the benefit of), but a spiritual awakening can be equally effective without using any formal therapeutic techniques or any external intervention. The sea change that can happen to one's perception, including perception of self, when events or experiences bring this about can change damaged lives instantly and completely. Such 'awakenings' happen all the time and when someone experiences such revelation it brings with it the emergence of an understanding so all encompassing that it repositions their life completely.

A word often used to describe such revelations is enlightenment.

Spirituality isn't religion and it does not require acceptance of the concept of a God though it can encompass this belief also. Whilst religions differ in their emphasis, their respective gods tend to have similar characteristics, usually demanding obedience and subservience. Religions invariably employ concepts of judgment and punishment and demand absolute adherence. They are primarily concerned with personal control, group membership and ritual, yet even within these artificial constructs many manage to find the spiritual connection required to change the direction of their lives.

So if spirituality doesn't mean religion then what is it? What relevance does it have to the issue of alcoholism?

Imagine for a moment that there is more to life than meets the eye. We have already explored how our behavior is determined by our perspective of the world around us. It isn't too much of a leap to imagine that there might be something else; something beyond our current understanding that is not easily definable. Many of us at have had the feeling that we are not simply the body we inhabit, that somehow there must be more. Perhaps some understanding of what the other part is could help us make more sense of our lives. Could such understanding also help to change habitual behavioral patterns that have developed over many years?

Religious conversions, near death experiences, mystical experiences, internal messaging, channeling and visions may all be forms of greater awareness. People who have experienced such powerful alterations in consciousness often make dramatic changes to the way they live and what they believe.

Religion is the cornerstone of the 12 step program of Alcoholics Anonymous as discussed earlier. In this instance, the associated spirituality promotes positive changes in people's lives. In other cases, spirituality, often in the form of religion, can be used as a justification for extremist, divisive and destructive behavior. How powerful must the message be to drive a young person with a comfortable life and close family to blow themselves up and intentionally take the lives of others through the deliberate act of a suicide bombing? You may understand the potential for good that a spiritual awareness can bring as well as the destructive power it can unleash when conjoined with religious doctrine.

Personal spiritual experience holds a truth that is uncontaminated by the motivations of man. People who have allowed a spiritual connection to permeate their lives help us recognize that it is a powerful catalyst for change particularly in the context of alcoholism.

So how might you go about seeking that spiritual connection? Do you join a Church, become a convert to a religion or simply integrate some meditative practice into your daily life. Firstly, you might want to consider your level of resistance before you could accept any particular version of spirituality. How high would you set the bar before you would feel able to bridge the belief gap? It does seem that it is the belief in something 'more' that is the key element. Does that belief need to be unquestionable for it to have the desired effect?

Certainly I have worked with a number of people who have tried the spiritual approach to overcome their addiction to drink. In some instances it has been a highly effective intervention and in others it hasn't helped at all. However, in the same way that paying your gym membership alone won't make you any fitter, joining a spiritually oriented group and singing along doesn't always promote enlightenment. If this approach is so far off your radar, just ignore it and find another way to work on your drinking problem?

Whatever your feeling is towards the concept of spirituality, it is a fact that thousands of people do acknowledge it and where these concepts are embraced, dramatic life changes can ensue.

There are other ways to seek spiritual enlightenment that you may not be aware of. I am also a contributing author to the book 'Memories of the Afterlife', published by Llewellyn, which is a collection of stories about people whose lives have changed as a result of a spiritual experience brought about under hypnosis and called LBL (Life Between Lives) spiritual regression. The process is one developed by Dr Michael Newton[22] and you can find out more about LBL, how it works and what it is designed to achieve at my website: www.nlp-hypnotherapy.biz

Summary

Having a spiritual element in your life can be beneficial. In fact, the evidence for the power of spiritual belief is overwhelming, so it is something worth pursuing if it is at all possible for you to embrace the concepts involved. Spiritual enlightenment can change behavior quickly and dramatically. There are many instances where individuals have undergone a sea change through finding their spiritual selves.

There are a variety of ways to seek enlightenment, including through religious practice but this is not the only way. Some need the formality of a group environment whereas others find comfort, relief and connectedness alone with themselves. There is no right way.

What seems to be important in creating change is the belief that we do not exist independently. That we are not alone and we have an existence beyond the physical limitations of our everyday lives.

The spiritual perspective, if taken on, helps overwrite invalid core beliefs about the self.

Chapter 12

Personal, social and political reflections

A complete change

I am not a recovering alcoholic I am fully recovered. Previously I wasn't destitute or drunk all the time but I couldn't do without alcohol. Now I have quite a different perspective on drinking. I know that I don't need it at all and the idea of never drinking again doesn't scare me. There has been a fundamental change in my perception. I now grasp, sometimes quite clearly, how powerful I can be and how much control I have over my life.

When I work with people on a personal level I encourage self awareness. The objective shouldn't be just to fix the alcohol problem alone, as you might fix a puncture, but to begin a journey of understanding and enlightenment.

Achieving control over your life requires you to have an awareness of how your body works and it helps to consider the latest ideas in biology that are starting to emerge. The control of behavior at the individual and cellular level is slowly beginning to be understood, but some of the newer concepts haven't yet permeated the mainstream so you have to seek them out.

My approach challenges the longstanding medical model dramatically and may create considerable resistance, especially where there are existing vested interests.

I was able to change my established and well managed relationship with alcohol because I allowed my knowledge and understanding to develop. That knowledge led to the most dramatic realization of all; that I had the power to change. Clients who also tread this path toward greater personal awareness find it becomes much easier to let go of crutches such as alcohol, reducing the importance they hold forever.

True change means that alcohol will never again be seen as a solution and whatever future events may occur, good or bad, the former patterns are unlikely to be reinstated. To be in that place, to have that mindset, represents true recovery. I don't believe it is possible to just remove an addiction as if it were a bad tooth. Addressing only the symptom can never fully solve the problem. However, there clearly is a need for practical interventions when the situation is so out of control that the necessary insight and awareness is swamped by the problem. When this is the case, I support the use of whatever method works to help the individual stop drinking and create a window of sobriety in order to address the root causes of the behavior. People I work with generally find that other aspects of their life also improve when they address their alcohol problem using my program. You might expect this to be the case where the alcohol addiction is symptomatic of underlying emotional issues. Typically, visible alcohol problems conceal other unhappiness because of their prominence. Other life issues that are connected to the same underlying cause may not be considered significant enough to address in isolation. Addressing the fundamental causes of emotional discomfort creates an improvement in these associated areas as well.

Counting the benefits

I've already mentioned some of the benefits that I personally experienced when I put drinking in its rightful place, but there were others that weren't so easy to spot.

I had more time to do things. It could be as much as eight hours a week. Periods of general lethargy, low level hangovers and daytime sleeping reduced dramatically. The new experience of being able and motivated to do other stuff was unexpected yet stimulating and satisfying. I recovered all the time I lost whereas before I would be recovering.

As I adjusted to this new sense of freedom, I found I could make good use of the time, get on with important work or tackle one of the many household tasks that would previously have been deferred to a weekend or until my wife lost patience (actually that still happens but I'm sure you get the point).

I noticed that I was more alert and awake than before. This really surprised me because I wasn't aware of how much of my energy was being squandered. In the past, although I wouldn't have been overtly drunk, I would have been much less enthusiastic to do anything because my concentration and motivation were markedly diminished.

I also had more money in my pocket. I didn't monitor it meticulously in the sense of putting aside money that I might have spent on alcohol. I just found that cash in my wallet lasted all week. The cost of the 'drinks' component of a meal was significantly less when we ate out. I worked out that I was spending about £200 (over $300.00) per month on alcohol. Such a net increase in disposable income really makes a difference.

It's really odd but drinking with friends always seems to work out being more expensive than the cost of your individual consumption. Weekends away that began with a carefully estimated cost often doubled regardless of the destination. Restaurants with sensibly priced food still managed to exceed cost expectations when the alcohol was added. This being said, the financial benefits don't really drive the agenda for most people. We really don't want everyone to know that the money is an issue and to be overly concerned with it can be embarrassing. After all, as committed members of the group we'll pay our way regardless of the cost so we don't think twice before ordering that extra bottle of wine.

Alcohol in society
Society, particularly in the UK recognizes that current alcohol consumption patterns are responsible for many social and economic problems. These range from disruptive, anti-social and violent behavior to the increasing cost of treating illnesses that

long term and excessive drinking causes. It is generally acknowledged that moderating alcohol use overall and minimizing the attraction of 'binge' drinking would have a beneficial effect upon society and governments are motivated to regularly introduce 'initiatives' purported to achieve these ends.

It is a tricky problem indeed. Apart from the extreme love of alcohol that seems to be part of the British psyche, and has been for hundreds of years, the trade in alcoholic beverages, in the UK, makes a very significant contribution to the exchequer, annually about 14 billion pounds sterling.[23] The ongoing balancing act is, therefore, how to reduce the harmful consumption of alcohol without affecting the income it generates.

The prevailing ideas and strategies of NICE,[24] a public body that has been asked to report on this problem include, attacking the product directly by introducing minimum pricing, tougher licensing laws, reducing the number of outlets and zero tolerance regarding alcohol related crime and anti-social behavior. Some of these ideas, if properly implemented, will directly address the problem but critically the proposal on minimum pricing seems to be more concerned with maintaining revenues than reducing drinking.

Simply increasing the price of alcohol doesn't necessarily have the fixed linear correlation with consumption over the longer term that such a policy presumes. There may be a short term effect but pricing objections will be overcome and we may see a specifically targeted increase in promotional activity accordingly.

The situation regarding taxation is not straightforward. It is a bit of a 'Catch 22'. If the government increased tax on alcohol by way of a minimum price it may, in the short term, receive similar income from an initial reduction in sales. As people become accustomed to the new prices, however, consumption may well increase leading to an increase in revenue. This makes it even harder to reduce sales in the future. If, on the other hand, the imposed price increase for alcohol goes ahead, without being associated with taxation, the beneficiary will be the alcohol industry.

A simple rule of thumb is that the more money there is in an industry the more attractive it becomes. We could face the irony of a minimum price that actually increases overall consumption in the medium and long term so for that reason I challenge whether it will be an effective policy.

It is important to remember that the national pattern of alcohol consumption is the sum of the perceptions and behaviors of each individual. Increasing prices doesn't address how people feel about alcohol and consequently will be limited in its impact of facilitating long term and real change.

The corporate world

Another approach already being employed is the 'top' down, 'drink responsibly' campaign.

Organizations, particularly those in the alcohol business, are incapable of expressing the motivations needed to present this message with sincerity. Businesses tend to exploit the regulatory and employment framework to their advantage to ensure maximum profits whilst paying lip service to such campaigns. It isn't enough simply to compel them to place a 'Drink Responsibly' message on their bottles and cans when that message itself is contradicted by everything else they do.

The pub landlord is not paid more by the brewery for selling less. The brewery area manager isn't set targets to achieve lower levels of public consumption and breweries don't reduce the rent for the pub managers if they underperform. Each component within the alcohol industry has a simple objective just like any other business and that is to sell more. Should we expect anything different - job security depends upon an income which is directly related to sales.

The industry sees the issues quite differently. To them the problem is just the serious alcoholics, and binge drinkers. They see huge market potential in slightly increasing the drinking habits of all those moderate drinkers – this is where the numbers are.

A way forward?

Moving the British drinking culture in the right direction would mean fewer problem drinkers, fewer hospital admissions, fewer deaths and fewer arrests for brawls, assaults and less domestic violence, road traffic accidents and drink-driving. It is an objective worth pursuing.

However, there are economic ramifications to reducing drinking behavior that need to be considered and addressed. Less drinking means lower alcohol sales and that will have an effect on the system as a whole. Sales are in fact slowing as I write this book, however, largely because of the effects of the recession and government spending cuts. So the trend is largely fortuitous and could easily reverse when times improve.

Lower national consumption would also result in fewer outlets. Less alcohol would be made and increased competition may result in a reduction in prices. A shrunken industry also means fewer jobs from the orchard to the cleaning supplier. It isn't possible to cut drinking behavior without an associated reduction in economic activity in associated sectors. Any plan to reduce our love of alcohol over the longer term must consider the effect such a reduction would have on employment and incorporate a strategy to replace those jobs over the same timescale.

How can a real reduction in overall alcohol use be achieved? There is not enough emphasis within the NICE 2010 public health guidelines about the need to challenge and change beliefs, neither does it explore how much smaller we as a society, want the alcohol business to be.

Consider the dramatic reduction in smoking in the last 60 years, a process that has accelerated over the last 30 years. The change in attitude has been staggering to the point where I can almost envisage a completely smoke-free society. The change owes a great deal to the demonstration of the clear association between smoking and severe health issues in addition to the strong support of government. Perhaps the same is possible with alcohol but, at the moment, I personally cannot envisage the possibility of an alcohol-free society in quite the same way. Clearly though, it is possible and there are many societies where alcohol is simply not a part of the culture and they are still enjoying life.

Recently, I watched an old film where the lead character smoked at work, in the office, over dinner, in conversation and whilst driving. I surprised myself by how I felt about these depictions. I found it quite disgusting and inconsiderate and the thought in my mind was "how can they not see that this is a revolting habit". I feel the same way in real life when someone smokes near me yet I was a smoker until a few years ago. I remember that at the time I felt entirely differently about it. If it is possible to feel so differently as an individual, clearly it must also be possible for similar changes to occur on a societal basis.

The key questions in my view are: How do we change attitudes enough to bring this about and over what timescale?

The 2010 NICE document *'Alcohol-use disorders: preventing harmful drinking'* in my opinion pays lip service to this issue. It tends to focus on short-term tactics rather than longer term thinking.

The wider societal problem is part of your problem. Not only does it support your addiction, it actively encourages it. Despite the fact that on an individual basis people can choose how to lead their lives, our society is still promoting unhealthy drinking. The personal devastation this problem creates shows up all over the system through crime, mortality and medical treatment statistics. At the moment our society seems to be tolerating alcohol abuse and promotes this toxic drug as a desirable and necessary part of life.

This has to change.

For the moment, the good news is that we can eliminate its influence on a personal level regardless of the wider society's perspective – and that has to be a message worth spreading.

Final thoughts

This book provides tried and tested ways of making these changes in your life but, central to all the advice is to be true to yourself and to try to develop deeper personal awareness. You can become fully responsible for your life and actions once you are aware that you are able to. The journey to reinforce your sense of self and strengthen the connections to those around you is a critical part of removing the obsession permanently.

Strive to extend your knowledge and strengthen your sense of control. When this happens the alcohol will simply become an unwelcome distraction.

If the approaches in this book don't get you to where you want to be, you will undoubtedly find another way if you persevere. I wish you good luck and encourage you to plan well, keep an open mind and be persistent.

Appendices

Appendix 1a

Definitions and classification

What is 'Alcohol dependence'?

Features of the 'Alcohol Dependence Syndrome', a term coined by Edwards and Gross in 1976, include:

- *A narrowing of the drinking repertoire (i.e. neglect of alternative pleasures or interests as a result of the alcohol use)*
- *Subjective awareness of a compulsion to drink (i.e. a strong desire to drink)*
- *Salience of drink-seeking behavior (i.e. a great deal of time is spent in activities related to acquiring, using or recovering from use of alcohol)*
- *Increased tolerance to alcohol (i.e. you require increased amounts to achieve the same effect)*
- *Repeated withdrawal symptoms*
- *Relief or avoidance of withdrawal symptoms by further drinking, and*
- *Rapid reinstatement after a period of abstinence*

Typically, people with severe alcohol dependency problems will experience significant *alcohol withdrawal* (see below) and may have formed the habit of drinking to avoid the withdrawal symptoms. Consequently, they may drink heavily on a daily basis over prolonged periods. It is estimated that 4% of adults in England are alcohol dependent.

'Psychological dependence' suggests that there are no physical withdrawal features with abrupt abstinence of use. 'Physiological dependence', usually a feature of more severe dependence, is indicated by the presence of withdrawal and tolerance to alcohol (see above list).

People with Physiological dependence will generally require medically-assisted alcohol withdrawal or 'detoxification', with up to a week of sedative, benzodiazepine medication to manage the symptoms. This can be done at hospital or in the community. Following detoxification, some will require a longer period (many months) in residential rehabilitation, something that may take time to organize and is expensive to fund.

If you fall into this category and think you require a detoxification +/- rehabilitation, it is essential to speak openly to your GP or local alcohol service for advice and support.

The notion of alcoholism as a 'disease' is centered on whether or not there is evidence of alcohol dependence. Consequently, the 'Alcohol Dependence Syndrome' has informed the main psychiatric diagnostic classification systems since. Other criteria of alcohol dependence that have been added into these classification systems over the years include:

- *Difficulty in controlling drinking, with a persistent desire or unsuccessful efforts to cut down*
- *Continuing to drink despite clear evidence of its harmful consequences (both physical and mental)*

What is 'Alcohol withdrawal'?

The 'Alcohol Withdrawal Syndrome' as it is commonly known, is a set of symptoms that manifest when alcohol is markedly reduced or stopped abruptly after a prolonged period of excessive consumption. It is due to the central nervous system being in a hyper excitable state. In rare cases it is a potentially fatal condition so it should be taken seriously.

Alcohol withdrawal is on a spectrum of severity ranging from mild symptoms, including sleep difficulties and low grade anxiety, to severe and life threatening symptoms such as convulsive seizures and a state called Delirium Tremens (commonly referred to as DT's) which is characterized by visual hallucinations, paranoia, seizures and severe agitation. The presence of withdrawal and the use of drink to relieve withdrawal is a good indicator of 'Physiological' rather than 'Psychological dependence'.

Common symptoms of withdrawal include:

- *Sweating*
- *Agitation and restlessness*
- *Anxiety and fear*
- *Tremor ('the shakes')*
- *Headaches*
- *Irritability*
- *Sleep disturbance (including nightmares)*
- *Gastrointestinal disturbance (including diarrhea, nausea and vomiting)*
- *Depression*
- *Confusion*
- *Cravings*

Sedative medications called benzodiazepines (e.g. 'Valium' or diazepam) are used to treat the symptoms of withdrawal during detoxification. Antipsychotics, anticonvulsants and certain vitamins (thiamine and folic acid) may also be required.

What is a 'safe' level of consumption?
The UK government recommends that adult men should not drink more that 4 units a day and women not more than 3 units on a regular basis (1995). The implication is that there should be some alcohol-free (or lower consumption) days every week. The advice on pregnancy is to abstain (2008).

In the UK 1 unit of alcohol is defined as 8g (or 10ml) of pure ethanol. A UK unit contains 2/3 of the quantity of ethanol compared to a standard drink in the United States.

The following is a guide to the average number of UK units in a variety of drinks:[25]

- 1 Pint of Stella Artois   2.3 Units
- 1 Bottle of Budweiser 330 ml: 1.7 Units
- 1 Pint of John Smiths: 2.3 Units
- 1 Typical can of lager: 2.2 Units
- 1 Standard glass of wine: 2.3 Units
- 1 Large glass of wine: 3.3 Units
- 1 shot of spirit: 0.9 Units

In 1986, The Royal College of Psychiatrists advised that men should drink less than 21 units / week and women less than 14 units / week. People who drink less than these recommended limits are considered to be at low risk of harm. People who drink more than this but have not yet experienced any alcohol-related harm are regarded as 'Hazardous drinkers' (World Health Organization), a definition based on research into alcohol-related mortality.

Drinking over 50 units of alcohol / week for men and over 35 units / week for women is regarded as 'definitely harmful' (Royal College 1986) and over 8 units / day in men and 6 units in women, according to the UK government, defines them as 'binge drinkers'.

In 2008, 21% of adult men drank between 22-50 units / week and 15% of women between 15-35 units / week. A further 7% of men and 5% of women were drinking above 50 and 35 units / week respectively.

Diagnostic classification systems – DSM IV and ICD 10

Alcohol use disorders are classified along with other psychiatric disorders in both of the two main diagnostic systems used today throughout the world:

- DSM IV (Diagnostic and Statistical Manual of mental disorders) is the US based system
- ICD IO (International Statistical Classification of Diseases) is the European equivalent, created by the World Health Organization

Both systems, which are very similar to each other, use a categorical, rule-based approach to diagnosis. They have evolved over the last half century or so with at least 4 separate updates, the most recent being in the early 1990s.

DSM IV has a diagnosis of *'Alcohol Abuse'* which refers to a "maladaptive pattern of substance abuse leading to clinically significant impairment or distress" and requires 1 of the following 4 criteria to be present:

1 Failure to fulfill major role obligations at work, school or home
2 Alcohol use in situations in which it is hazardous
3 Alcohol-related legal problems
4 Continued use despite repeated persistent/recurrent social or interpersonal problems.

It also has a diagnosis of *'Alcohol Dependence'* which trumps the Alcohol abuse diagnosis and broadly maps against the dependence criteria listed above requiring at least 3 of 7 criteria to be present at any time in a 12 month period. It has specifiers for course (e.g. early/full remission) and physiological dependence (i.e. tolerance or withdrawal).

ICD 10 has a diagnosis of *'Harmful use'* which identifies a pattern of use that, specifically, has already caused mental or physical damage (i.e. there is clear evidence of alcohol-related harm). Physical problems include liver disease and heart disease.

Mental problems include depression, anxiety disorders and cognitive impairment. The definition excludes those with alcohol dependence. Harmful drinkers are usually drinking above recommended maximum levels. It is quite different from the DSM IV conception of abuse.

ICD 10 also has a diagnosis of *'Alcohol Dependence'* which much like DSM IV, requires 3 out of 6 (not 7) symptoms to be present at any time in a 12 month period to meet the diagnostic threshold. The symptoms are similar but notably different from those listed in DSM IV but both are heavily influenced by Edwards and Gross' 'Alcohol Dependence Syndrome' (1976).

The term *'Hazardous use'* was also coined by the WHO but it does not appear in ICD 10 (although it was present in the draft version). It indicates 'a pattern of use that increases the risk of harmful consequences to the user.....in contrast to harmful use, hazardous use refers to patterns of use that are of public health significance despite the absence of any current disorder in the individual user'. The term continues to be used by the WHO in its public health program so it warrants a mention.

It is important to realize that alcohol-related problems are not as clearly classified as many other psychiatric illnesses. What sets them apart is that these conditions are associated with a degree of volition. The sufferer must seek out and consume alcohol on a regular basis in order to develop the illness. This is a distinct difference from a condition such as schizophrenia. Classifying one's volitional behavior as a disease is controversial.

Both classification systems are based on the medical model thereby implying a disease state. The more severe end of the spectrum e.g. physiological dependence is easier to conceptualize as a disease. With less severe forms e.g. alcohol abuse, this is not so clear cut.

In summary, although the modern diagnostic system is the accepted and mainstream approach for classifying alcohol disorders, unresolved controversies include the behavioral nature of the disorder, the obvious heterogeneity (individual variation) in the population and the high rates of psychiatric co-morbidity, all suggesting that the alcohol problem may be secondary to something else.

Subgroups of 'Alcoholics'

There have been various attempts to classify 'alcoholics' into sub-groups or typologies. There have been one-dimensional typologies based on **gender, family history, age of onset** and **drinking pattern**.

Probably the most influential sub-group system in terms of generating research was the **TYPE 1 / TYPE 2** divide. This came out of a Swedish study conducted by Cloninger in 1981, which has since been shown to have various methodological flaws. The study actually refers to Type 1 and 2 families, not the drinkers themselves, but the sub-grouping has since been applied to the individual.

- *Type 1 alcoholism* includes males only and is characterized by early age of onset, impulsivity and anti-social person-ality traits.
- *Type 2 alcoholism* includes both males and females, has a later age of onset and is associated with anxiety personality traits.

The latest typology to generate interest is the **TYPE A/B system**. It has a total of 17 variables broken down into these 4 domains:

1 Indicators of vulnerability and risk
2 Severity of dependence
3 Chronicity and consequences of drinking
4 Psychopathology

Broadly speaking, this model has been supported by the research and it is beginning to replace the Type 1/Type 2 system as the more commonly researched typology. Its critics argue that it may simply reflect a continuum of severity of alcohol dependence so the search is still out for an accurate model to describe the heterogeneity (or differences between individuals) in populations of drinkers.

Appendix 1b

Psychological therapies

Psychological therapies considered for inclusion in the new NICE guideline (2011) on alcohol:

Brief interventions (planned only)
- e.g. Psychoeducational and motivational techniques

Self-help based treatments
- Brief self-help interventions (including guided self help / bibliotherapy)

Twelve-Step facilitation
- Cognitive Behavioral-based therapies
- Standard Cognitive Behavior Therapy (CBT)
- Coping Skills
- Social Skills Training
- Relapse Prevention

Behavioral Therapies
- Cue Exposure
- Behavioral Self-Control Training
- Contingency Management
- Aversion Therapy

Motivational Enhancement Therapy
- Social Network and Environment Based Therapies
- Social Behavior and Network Therapy
- The Community Reinforcement Approach

Counseling
- Couples Therapy (including behavioral couples therapy and other variants of couples therapy)

Family-based Interventions
- Functional Family Therapy
- Brief Strategic Family Therapy
- Multi-systematic Therapy
- 5 Step Family Interventions
- Multi Dimensional Family Therapy
- Community Reinforcement and Family Training

Psychodynamic Therapy
- Short-term Psychodynamic Intervention
- Supportive Expressive Psychotherapy

Physical therapies such as Meditation and Acupuncture are also covered in the guideline.

Appendix I c

Motivational Enhancement Therapy and Cognitive Behavioral Therapy

Motivational Interviewing (MI) and Motivational Enhancement Therapy (MET)

MI is a therapeutic model developed by psychologists Miller and Rollnick. It is a useful set of techniques (sometimes referred to simply as an 'interpersonal style') that have the aim of creating rapport and a sense of partnership with the client. This is facilitated through a focus on empathy and a very permissive and accepting stance. At the same time the therapist is tasked with identifying and gently exploring discrepancies in the client's narrative and commenting on any ambivalence to change that presents itself. Ambivalence is the expression of a conflict between two courses of action and in MI its acknowledgement is encouraged but not forced. Sometimes verbal expression of the internal conflict facilitates some degree of resolution in itself. However, a key therapeutic objective of the technique is to engage and cultivate the client's motivation to change, with the therapist being highly attentive and responsive to the client's verbal and non-verbal feedback.

Motivational Interviewing is non-judgmental and non-instructive and it inherently avoids confrontation with the client. The advice given to the therapist is to 'roll with resistance', conceptualizing reluctance as a natural part of the process. In fact, any resistance expressed by the client is seen to reflect the therapist's behavior more than the clients, indicating that they may need to 'pull back' a little. In short, MI is about, exploring the problem behavior honestly and openly, at a pace determined by the client, creating both awareness of the potential pitfalls and risks of their ongoing use, whilst nurturing a picture of an alternative, brighter future. It is also about empowering the client, fostering autonomy and a sense of self-efficacy. It relies heavily on 'mobilizing the client's intrinsic values and goals to stimulate behavior change'. The assumption in Motivational Interviewing is that lack of resolve is the primary obstacle to change. Once this has been overcome there may or may not be a need for further intervention. There is a well known adaption of MI called Motivational Enhancement Therapy, which typically consists of four sessions of focused and structured work. There is good evidence for the approach in substance misuse and other areas but many see it as a tool or a style, better used as an adjunct rather than a therapy in its own right.

Cognitive Behavioral Therapy (CBT)

CBT is a well known, psychotherapeutic approach that is primarily focused on understanding and modifying one's thoughts (cognitions), emotions and behavior. It can be used individually, with couples and in group settings. It is systematic, time-limited (often brief), goal-directed and functions very much in the 'here and now'. The techniques are often manualized with specific, suggested protocols for different problems.

CBT is in fact an amalgamation of a diverse range of techniques drawn from *cognitive therapy* and *behavioral therapy*, two quite different ways of tackling problems but which share a commonality in that they both concentrate on the present difficulties without unearthing too much from the past. Different therapists have different orientations. Some are more 'cognitive', focused primarily on the thinking processes at play and their connection with the emotions, employing standard techniques to challenge, 'reframe' and 'restructure' dysfunctional thought patterns. Others are more interested in the individual's behavior, using techniques such as 'exposure' and 'repeated practice' to facilitate change. CBT's effectiveness has been demonstrated for a wide variety of different problems including mood and anxiety disorders, eating disorders and substance misuse problems. NICE (The National Institute for Health and Clinical Excellence) recommends CBT as the gold standard treatment for a number of mental health diagnoses.

As a result of the very scientific and research-orientated ethos of the CBT camp, which consists primarily of mainstream psychologists, it has been particularly effective at conducting and publishing good quality trials which have, on the whole, shown positive outcomes, favoring the approach over standard therapy. The UK government has recently put its weight behind the CBT 'revolution', allocating huge financial resource for training a large cohort of new therapists using quite a standardized approach. Many believe that this 'CBT cures all' mentality narrows the frame, hinders therapeutic creativity and neglects to recognize new and innovative approaches, particularly those that involve the body, and those that may have a less established evidence-base at the current time. The onus is clearly on the critics to get moving with the research but initiating research in this area can create its own problems. Opponents to the model argue that just because it has been shown to be 'effective' in studies, it doesn't necessarily mean it is the only way or the best way to approach problems.

The CBT model conceptualizes substance misuse disorders as learned behaviors, acquired through repeated exposure. The learning is either by *association* (the basis of Classical conditioning as discussed above) which is interested in substance-related cues or by *consequence* (otherwise known as Operant conditioning) which is concerned with the reinforcing nature of the 'high'. Much of the treatment is derived directly from these two models. For example, the technique 'cue exposure' involves identifying the conditioned triggers (or cues) and exposing the client to them repeatedly, unpaired with the substance, until the trigger loses its impact.

A primary task in treatment is to identify the specific needs being met by the substance and then to help the client develop new 'coping skills' to meet those needs in alternative ways. The idea is that these new skills are employed in the face of a craving and over time they will become more natural responses. 'Skills' can be seen as being either client-focused or interpersonal. Client-focused skills may include *techniques for managing cravings and drink related thoughts, tackling negative thinking, anger management, decision making, problems solving, contingency and crisis planning, recognizing relapse indicators, relaxation skills, filling free time* etc. Interpersonal skill may include *learning to decline substances, general assertiveness, managing criticism, relationships and communication skills, optimizing support and social networks.* There is quite a strong emphasis on Relapse Prevention work.

CBT is undoubtedly helpful and is an important contribution to the debate. In fact, many of the newer approaches have been shown to have a very strong CBT underpinning. However, CBT does rely quite heavily on identifying and navigating around problems or rationalizing them away. Given time these 'conscious' changes can, and often do, translate into real change at the subconscious level, particularly in more motivated clients. However, in many cases these new ways of thinking about behavioral modifications get a little tedious and energy consuming and after the novelty has worn off, particularly at times of stress, much of the new learning is dropped or disregarded, allowing the underlying, unresolved problem to resurface. CBT seems to be slowly moving towards an acknowledgement of the importance of the body and its role in processing of emotions but it is still very early days.

Appendix 2

Introducing the hypnosis audio files

About the audio files

I have created a number of audio files to help you make fundamental changes to your drinking behavior at the subconscious
level. They are available at:

www.thesophisticatedalcoholic.com

And are included as a part of the program at:

www.control-your-drinking.co.uk

I thought it would be helpful to explain a little more about how
these audio files can work for you.

Many people just buy them and use them because the audio
files are available as MP3 downloads and on CD and the website
has all the information you need. Some people achieve their goals
simply by listening to the recordings. Nearly all the comments I
have received from people are positive and I do know that many
have removed alcohol from their lives as a result.

To get the maximum benefit from the recordings always
ensure you are comfortable, free of interruption and not doing
anything else at the time. Specifically, do not listen whilst
driving. The recordings are designed to be heard through stereo
headphones. They utilize the left and right channels in a unique
way to aid relaxation and the effect isn't noticeable if you listen
through normal speakers.

'Can I be hypnotized?' audio series

This series will help you determine how hypnosis and suggestion might work for you. They begin with a sample suggestion that your subconscious mind can work with. Regard the audios as a bit of fun, just to see how it works. It is an excellent way to begin to learn how to use relaxation to your advantage.

Specific issues are not targeted in this series so most people should have minimal or no resistance to the relaxation or the suggestions.

I would advise you to familiarize yourself with the synopsis of each audio before downloading.

The hypnotic inductions move from a direct to a more permissive approach. To assess their effectiveness consider how relaxed they make you feel. You will probably be aware of everything around you during the process because your conscious mind will remain on-line.

Part I

This 13-minute audio file does not require you to enter a hypnotic trance at all. It simply offers the suggestion that your finger will lift without you having to do it consciously.

It is in your subconscious mind where changes are made with hypnosis. It is the part of your mind that will respond to the suggestion that your finger will rise.

This isn't really true hypnosis, it is merely a suggestion. The suggestion is direct, simple to understand, easy to do and non-threatening. It isn't important to you whether your finger moves or not so there is no reason not to comply. It is inherently possible because you can easily lift a finger and the finger will probably comply if the audio is listened to with an open mind.

When suggestions challenge belief they become subject to the conscious critique and unconscious obstruction. If, for example, the suggestion was to stop drinking it would probably have a limited effect. If that suggestion was given in the form of a direct instruction it would most probably fall flat immediately. If, on the other hand, it was well presented, aligned with beliefs you already hold and reinforced with new information about the dangers of alcohol it might last a week. Telling people to stop drinking, even under hypnosis, is rarely a permanent solution.

Successful long term change requires that the decisions come from the client themselves. The truly powerful contribution hypnosis makes is to elicit the desired changes from the client using structured language and seemingly unrelated examples called 'metaphors'.

Part 2
Part two lasts for about 10 minutes and uses a technique called 'direct induction' (not to be confused with 'direct suggestion') to bring about the relaxed state called hypnotic trance. It involves focusing on a single point for a period which helps relaxation. The benefit of direct induction is that it is relatively quick. The downside is that fewer people respond well to this form of induction and it takes considerable experience to determine who can or who can't, before one can decide which to use.

Part 3
Part three lasts for about 30 minutes and uses an 'indirect induction'. This is the process generally used by hypnotherapists because almost everyone achieves the level of relaxation required. Indirect inductions work best if they don't threaten existing beliefs. Often phrases such as "you may feel a lightness or a heaviness or no change at all" are employed simply because they avoid dispute by covering all options. However, if lightness or heaviness, or even 'no change' is a conclusion of the client they associate that feeling with the process itself and it acts to support the belief that hypnosis is taking place. The client does not associate the all-encompassing nature of the original statement

with their direct experience of one part of it.

Part 4

Part four lasts for about 20 minutes and is also an indirect induction but with a difference. It is used for people who have difficulty in achieving the necessary degree of relaxation. This approach introduces an element of purposeful confusion causing your conscious mind to focus on working out what has just been said, allowing the subconscious to become more receptive to suggestion.

The 'Alcohol Control' audio series

Alcohol Control I

Alcohol Control is a 31 minute complete hypnosis session. It challenges current perceptions about alcohol and alcohol related behavior. It employs strong direct and indirect suggestion, emphasizing the downsides of alcohol and seeking to reinforce your existing negative view of it to such a point that you will feel uncomfortable by continuing to drink heavily. I usually recommend this one first.

Alcohol Control II

Alcohol Control II is a 24 minute complete hypnosis session and follows a more permissive strategy. It employs metaphor and suggests structures that reinforce the sense that change is effectively a re-wiring of the brain. It addresses beliefs and fears about identity that, in themselves, are powerful opponents to change.

It also introduces the concept of self-permission. At some point everyone contemplating changes that will affect personal identity will also have to feel it's ok to be different in that way. It provides mechanisms, metaphor and suggestion, direct and indirect, to allow you to permit yourself to change.

Appendix 3

Alcohol Control I hypnosis script

Before listening

Read through this section before listening to the audio because it will help you to make an assessment of where you are now with your alcohol problem and where you will be.

I describe now a simple diagram that will help you to assess the degree of your problem, monitor improvement and make it psychologically easier to change.

On a piece of paper draw a circle approximately the size of an orange. Dissect the circle with a straight line from top to bottom and then from left to right. You should now have four sections within the circle. Dissect each of these with a line across leaving you with eight sections. Number these sections outside of the circle from 1 – 8.

Each section represents the degree of your relationship with alcohol. Section 1 representing low or zero alcohol use and section 8 representing very high consumption levels.

Think a moment then draw a small circle about the size of a pea inside the section that best represents your relationship with alcohol. With a marker pen black out all the sections with a higher number and also black out around your pea size circle. When your relationship with alcohol diminishes, redraw the little circle in a new and available lower numbered section and completely black out the section it came from.

Place the sheet of paper somewhere where you will always see it, perhaps on the fridge and perhaps another copy on the drinks cabinet, or the bathroom mirror, you choose. This is your reminder of your progress.

Pre-talk

Hello, my name is David Allen and I have produced this audio program to help you change the way you think and feel about alcohol and your relationship with it.

Before we move on make sure you are in a comfortable position and won't be disturbed for a while. You will notice that as you listen to my words you will feel very comfortable and relaxed and that this pleasant sensation will continue right through to the end of the recording.

Now, using a recorded hypnotic audio file is an easy and cheap way to change your life for the better.

I have produced a number of these recordings over the years that many people have found helpful and you can find these at:

www.thesophisticatedalcoholic.com

Hypnosis audio files are completely safe to listen to and can do no harm, but make sure you take time out for yourself specially to do this and do not listen if you are doing something else that requires your concentration at the same time and particularly not whilst driving.

Just listening will help you relax sufficiently for you to change the way you feel about alcohol and you can play it as many times as you want.

It is likely that you are listening to this audio because you have become concerned that you are drinking too much. You probably want to drink less or you may have decided that you do not need it at all, but whichever it is this hypnotic process will help you get to where you want to be.

The process of hypnosis is self regulating. You cannot suddenly become tee total if all you wanted was to reduce your drinking. Your subconscious mind knows exactly what you want to do and it will make the changes you want.

As the brain begins to relax and slow down the energy waves it produces change in nature and it is this change that helps your subconscious mind to re-wire itself so that you will just feel differently about alcohol and restore a balance that has been lost.

Whilst your subconscious mind is listening to my words and making the changes you want; the conscious part of you will still be there, a bit like a bystander, just observing what is going on, just watching and listening.

Before we begin the relaxation process let's just look at some reasons why alcohol is now a problem.

You have been, and still are under extreme pressure to drink alcohol. There is almost no restriction on the amount of money spent on its promotion and, in common with most heavily advertised items, none of it is really true.

Advertising is about selling and is extremely effective whether you consciously watch it or not. Even if you aren't paying attention it still affects how you think and feel and with the solitary purpose of getting you to drink more.

Over time and with constant repetition you form firm beliefs about drinking and its place in your life that aren't true, yet they become so entrenched they seem to be true. This audio will sharpen your awareness and cause you to re-evaluate the role of alcohol in your life and to develop a kind of immunity to its unremitting promotion.

You already know that drinking brings you all sorts of problems including the adverse effects on health and wellbeing, career, relationships and perhaps your behavior as well.

After all it is a drug that affects the way you think, feel and behave just like any other recreational narcotic. You have already decided that enough is enough and things have to change and you may already feel some anger because of the grip this drug has upon you and you can allow that anger to grow because it will help you to see it for what it is.

Whether you want to just drink less, rarely or not at all may not be readily apparent now even though you have probably thought about just where you want to be but that can so easily change when your understanding changes but I can assure you that whatever level you choose it will be because that is what you want to do.

Induction

Now it's quite likely that as I've been talking to you some relaxation will have already have begun and you may already feel really comfortable and sort of sleepy in a strange kind of way. You may also have already closed your eyes or kept them open but the more you listen to my words the more comfortable it will seem to just allow them to close, but it doesn't really matter if they stay open, though feeling heavy, or they close because you can do this in any way you want.

So there really is nothing for you to do other than to relax and breathe in a quiet and subtle manner though you could always take a deep breath as well if you wanted to.

You may even decide to adjust your position from time to time and that's fine because you will retain an awareness of your surroundings though the most important thing is to listen to me because you will hear my voice clearly and understand me easily even though you may find it all too much bother to make sense of the meaning of my words in a conscious and rational kind of way.

At this point you may feel very sleepy as well as relaxed and that's ok because you can just enjoy that as you won't sleep as you would do at night and you can easily tell that is the case because you can always hear me really clearly even if you happen to be thinking about something else at the time.

Deepening

Just to help you even more I'm going to count down from 10 to 1 and as I do that I want you to imagine yourself, just imagine that you are going deeper and deeper with each count down as I begin to count now.

10, 9, 8, 7, 6, 5, 4, 3, 2, 1

I want you to think what it's like travelling. You might imagine a car journey you took recently or perhaps a long time ago or a bus ride or train trip or even when you went to a quite different place for a holiday.

You might think that life is also a journey because of all the similarities there are like having a beginning and end and the fact that all sorts of decisions have to be taken from time to time and you might be able to think of many more quite similar things though that's not too important right now.

So imagine that you are just driving somewhere. It doesn't matter if you don't drive because everyone has been in a car or a bus or perhaps ridden a bike and you can imagine yourself as the driver and notice all the things in it that you can decide about.

Of course you usually decide where you want to go but even before then there are all sorts of things we usually don't even think about that are a part of any car journey. Some people unlock the car from inside the house, you know, through the window and some from outside the garage if you are one of those people who can get their car inside the garage. Others wait until they are about to open the door before unlocking so you can see that there are many ways to just unlock the car before even getting in it.

Driving is such a natural process when you have learned to do it and have had some practice. The co-ordination is exceptional when you approach a corner and use your feet to operate the pedals with a heavy foot or a light foot then change the gear and switching on the indicator as well as turning the wheel to guide the car along exactly the right path and all of this done without any conscious thought whatsoever. It's really interesting that even when an unexpected event happens whilst you are doing all of this it is immediately incorporated into the scene and new actions not before needed are now called into play.

All of these actions happening automatically, even the surprise ones. Like when you turn a corner and someone partially steps into the road as if to cross but without paying enough attention and then notices you turning toward them and a whole series of actions just arise as you brake without thinking which pedal to press first and the pedestrian jerks back onto the pavement without any prior knowledge that they were going to do that yet the decision to act and the actions themselves just happened.

Have you ever wondered how long or how heavy a thought is? To decide to do something may only take a fraction of a second like when you decide to brake suddenly and may or may not be influenced by the difficulty of the action. In this case the actions were what we often call responses where a learned operation stored deep within the subconscious mind is called into play in the same way as we replay habitual behavior yet other actions may be seen to be more difficult but the decision, I mean that initial thought process can still be immediate and weigh nothing yet it precipitates lots of actions that equally may or may not require lots of effort.

It interesting to notice how many times we unlock the car, get into it, sit behind the wheel, start the engine, choose a gear either to go forwards or backwards and all sorts of other routine things that you could change if you wanted to. Maybe to do them in a different order or to do some a bit less and some a bit more or even to omit some actions altogether though you probably wouldn't want to omit checking your mirrors or looking behind you as you pull out.

Sometimes and it may be on a longer journey or a short one, a foot might fall asleep or feel heavier or lighter or a sensation may appear like the itching of a foot underneath the shoe where it's really difficult to scratch and you might try all kinds of strange movements to satisfy this itching without having to stop or do anything you feel would be unsafe. Once your attention is taken or you stop and remove the shoe to really give this a good scratch it just goes away and you might be left wondering why it began in the first place because that's a very interesting question.

Noticing and appreciating go together and now you will be deeply relaxed allowing each breath to take you deeper and deeper and you might be thinking about driving or something else altogether and when you do you might think that some driving is easy and some more difficult though you can choose to go to the coast on a bank holiday and also change that decision if it might get much worse than you thought and you may decide that you just don't need that today.

I'm going to be quiet for a few moments now and during that time I would like you to imagine, just imagine yourself drifting deeper and deeper into a very pleasant state of relaxation and when you are sufficiently deep you will know and I will know because you will find yourself taking two nice deep breaths.

Suggestions

Now you are deeply and pleasantly relaxed though you can still adjust your position if you are uncomfortable and just enjoy that sense of quiet reflection though still very much in control.

This is a time now for you to consider the kind of life you want.

A time of quiet periods, with no words from me and these can be times to allow yourself to drift even deeper into the trance and allow your subconscious to make the changes you want.

30 Second Pause.

Alcohol abuses you rather than you it.

30 Second Pause

On balance alcohol causes more grief than it gives pleasure.

30 Second Pause

Alcohol steals water from your body and in this sense it is a thief.

30 Second Pause

Doesn't it annoy you that this mind altering drug has such a grip on you and that you allow it to take control?

30 Second Pause

How can something so unnecessary become so important?

30 Second Pause

It's easy to change.

30 Second Pause

You know that the unremitting promotion of alcohol relies entirely on lies.

30 Second Pause

Excess usage of alcohol damages lives in so many ways.

30 Second Pause

Why is it that the significant health risks of alcohol are so underplayed?

30 Second Pause

It's easy to change.

30 Second Pause

Allow your subconscious mind to work on these issues whilst I tell you a story.

Metaphor

Imagine that you are at the edge of a beautiful field, perhaps standing by the edge of the road or in a field next door which is not important and the field can be any kind of field you might want it to be, perhaps a corn field with the corn not yet fully grown or even a field of flowers gently blowing in the warm and comfortable breeze.

There is a path running alongside the edge of this field that I want you to walk along just at a comfortable pace, just follow the path enjoying the warmth of the air on this beautiful day feeling so good and so relaxed.

The path crosses into another field and you can climb over the stile into this new field and continue along the path which is well worn so others come this way as well perhaps because of the beauty of this place but that doesn't matter right now. Ahead there is a small footbridge that crosses a stream and you can pause for a moment on the middle of this little bridge looking down at the crystal clear shallow water hurrying past each obstacle as if it were important for each molecule of water to get there first. This natural and peaceful process with its constant cleaning of the stones and pebbles will help you to become more relaxed as you begin to understand how everything can fit together so perfectly.

As you continue on your way the sound of the stream lessens. Up ahead there is an old building, a monument of times past where some of the original stone work still exists and other parts have been refurbished. Everything is so well tended, the grass is neat and short and flower beds adorn the cobbled pathways. It's as if it's being allowed to age but with great care and attention as it does so.

There is an entrance doorway which is open and welcoming for all who want to visit this peaceful place and as you enter there appears a light that envelopes you completely with warmth and protection and a very special feeling comes over your entire body.

Often there are times when it just seems right to make a change, perhaps when we feel well and secure or maybe at other times but it does happen so you can allow this feeling of secure comfort to wash over you completely and enjoy the feeling of deep comfort and relaxation.

As you continue to experience this feeling you may feel this to be an opportunity to completely change your perspective on alcohol as something which does not need to be a part of your life. Somehow at times like these fundamental changes can occur to the essence of whom you really are, to your sense of self that some call the soul and others the spirit. You can change subconscious beliefs and perceptions and feel as if it is the easiest thing in the world to do and it is at times like these when destructive behaviors can be eradicated forever and you can choose to do this now with alcohol and remove its misplaced importance from your life completely and it can be as if it were never an issue at all.

As you leave this place take with you these feelings of strength and power and control and return the way you came. When you go over the small footbridge you can again notice the symmetry of the universe expressed in the superficially random haste of each molecule of water as it continues its journey to complete the circle of existence.

Now you can look forward to your future with renewed motivation and vigor and remember this place for what it has helped you to achieve.

Surfacing from the trance state

Before you allow yourself to drift back up completely into wakeful conscious awareness it may be useful to use this time to think about what you have experienced and how good you will feel because you have achieved what you want.

That's right, take some time now, a brief time that seems to be a long time to review and plan at some level of awareness the things that have changed and those further changes that may take place later on.

You can use that time now because in a few moments from now when you drift up and awaken it may be interesting for you to think of this drifting relaxed state of mind where thoughts drift like dreams that can enter awareness for only a short time and then disappear.

Perhaps they drift through the mind whilst some are left behind to be utilized later on and others are remembered or seem to be remembered at first but then become more and more distant, forgotten over time and the entire experience can seem so far away.

As your subconscious mind protects your conscious mind and leaves those things behind, forgotten but remembered too. And time changes too so you can know and understand this experience and how it has helped you to get to where you want to be.

And you may begin to know that what seemed to take a short time turned out to be a long time or what seemed a long time was really no time at all.

Just take these last few moments to make certain that the changes have been thoroughly implemented, that the processes have completed and that your perspective has altered.

So as the subconscious mind allows the conscious mind to become more aware of sounds and other external stimuli, sensations in arms and legs you can drift up to the surface of wakeful awareness.

Drifting up now, and as I count from 1 to 5 you will move closer and closer to wakeful awareness as each number is heard. Counting now 1...2...3...4...5. And the eyes are allowed to open now, that's right eyes open and wakeful awareness returns quite completely. Now!

Appendix 4

Alcohol Control II hypnosis script

Induction

Just take a little time to position your body so that you feel poised and balanced, comfortable and at ease.

Take a few moments to do this. Adjust your head so that you are comfortable, your back, your arms, your legs. As we continue, if you would like to change your position to become even more comfortable then you can do that.

And so we begin. Pick a spot somewhere in front of you that you can see easily and continue to look at that spot as I talk to you.

It may be a wallpaper pattern, or a door handle or the corner of a frame or anything at all but keep looking at it as I speak to you, give it your full visual attention whilst and at the same time you give me your full audio attention.

Already as you are looking at that spot you may begin to perceive some very subtle changes in your vision.

You may notice that the spot becomes very easy to see, you may also notice that the periphery of your vision surrounding that spot may begin to get hazy.

The more you focus your entire visual attention on that spot the more the rest of your vision will move out of focus.

What is interesting about this is that as you concentrate on just that spot your eyes will begin to feel a little heavier. You may have already noticed this heaviness becoming more and more difficult to ignore and that the heaviness may also be accompanied with a feeling of sleepiness, a sort of strange tiredness becoming more and more noticeable as you continue to focus on that spot.

That's right, feeling heavier and heavier, sleepier and sleepier, though you can still hear me clearly and will be able to do that throughout the entire process.

As you continue to focus on that spot your eyes will continue to tire yet you can also feel a quiet comfort in just allowing the occasional blink to happen even though a little more effort is now needed to keep those eyes open.

Soon you will just decide that it would be more comfortable for you to allow your eyes to close and when you feel that you can just do it. In fact, do that now and allow your eyes to fall shut. Feel just how peaceful and comfortable that is. Begin to notice other sensations in your body that perhaps were there all the time but just out of your range of perception.

Now it's strange and rather interesting to observe that although you have felt sleepy and tired you are not asleep as you might be at night even though your mind is beginning to slow down but just resting at that comfortable place just before complete sleep, you can easily tell that is the case because you can hear me and the other sounds around you just as if you were wide awake.

In the same way that you focused your visual attention on the spot earlier you can now focus your auditory attention on just my voice.

There may be other sounds around you and other sounds may appear from time to time but because they are not important to you at this time they will, like the hazy visual periphery that you have already experienced, fade into the background.

All that is important to you at this time is my voice and words that are directed only to you. It's really comforting to know that you only need listen to me when I'm talking to you and you don't even have to bother to respond in any way to other sounds that may occur from time to time.

You may also notice how easy it is now to tune into the rhythm of your breathing, noticing that when you are still, your body adopts a breathing rhythm which is most beneficial to you at this time.

As you inhale and exhale your chest moves with the rhythm, quite noticeably when you breathe in deeply yet quietly and subconsciously when you slow everything down to that comfortable relaxation.

An interesting thing is that your breathing is quite automatic and just happens exactly at the rate you need it to without you having to even think about it yet also you can take direct control whenever you wish, just like when you decide to take a deep breath, perhaps to calm or to slow your heartbeat which deep controlled breaths can do quite easily.

As you become more and more at ease you will notice that each breath in, whether that be large or small, will deepen your relaxation and each breath out takes with it tension and anxiety from your body and you may feel a heaviness or lightness resulting from a further relaxing of every muscle. Each muscle in your body losing all tension as you continue to drift deeper and deeper into this pleasantly relaxed state.

You can actually check around your body to see if any muscles are still tense or not quite completely relaxed and if you find any, you can use your breathing to let that tension out, so take a moment or two to take a tour of your body and just see if you can notice any remaining tension and if you do you can let yourself breathe out through that part so the tension can leave right away.

You may also notice that your heartbeat becomes more regular and consistent along with your breathing as you continue to relax even more.

A regular even rhythm achieving what we call coherence where you are deeply relaxed. Your breathing and your heart rate is perhaps almost imperceptible so you may only really sense it on a cellular level, deep inside. The coherence adds to the effectiveness of your entire system, so whilst quiet and slow its benefits to you are magnified in all aspects.

You may also notice that as I continue to talk to you, thoughts drift through your mind freely and sometimes with no clear connection, just appearing, that's fine.

You can feel the rhythm of your thoughts without having to bother to pick any one out as they drift in and out of your mind. Sometimes they just don't appear but it doesn't matter because everyone has these thoughts even though they are still deeply relaxed.

Know that at this time there is nothing you need to do or change or even think about.

You may even feel that the effort it takes to be aware of the sound of my voice or the meaning of my words may almost seem to be too much effort to bother making.

It's so much easier to just relax and enjoy that letting go. All you really have to do is just breathe. Just feel and experience the rhythm in your body.

Feeling a sense of comfortable stillness. Feeling a sense of quiet deep within you. Allowing your subconscious mind to work freely and easily in this process of healing.

Deepening

As you are about to become ready I'm going to count down from 10 to 1. When I do this I want you to imagine yourself, just imagine that you are drifting deeper and deeper into the trance with each count, as you do this you will notice yourself becoming more and more at one with your body being able to influence how it might work better for you now and at any other time.

10, 9, 8, 7, 6, 5, 4, 3, 2, 1.

That's right, deeply and comfortably relaxed.

Now as you continue to relax and drift in your thoughts, that's right, as you notice your breathing, more and more at ease now, deeper and deeper with each breath.

I want you to find for yourself a wonderful place, a sanctuary in your mind where you can be when you listen to my words. A place that will help you to put things in perspective and you will probably be surprised as to how well you can do this and how helpful it can be.

If you want to you can just follow me into a peaceful place and stay there or go to wherever you want with just a thought.

Perhaps you might want to come with me to begin with and to do that just visualize, feel or imagine yourself now on the porch or veranda of a large house, at the top of a classically tiled flight of steps leading down into the most beautiful walled garden you have ever seen.

Slowly make your way down the steps into the garden and just imagine yourself going deeper and deeper with each step down.

When you reach the bottom of the steps, go into the garden and wonder at its beauty and tranquility.

There are flowers, trees, a pond and waterfall and you may actually be able to hear the flow of the water as it cascades over pebbles and stones and back to the pond from whence it came.

It is a beautiful day, the sky is clear and blue and you can feel the warm breeze brushing your face. This is a place of complete peace and a place you can relax and from here you can also allow your mind to roam and return at will, from here you can go wherever you want to go and return whenever you want to return.

There are many places to sit and relax in this calm peaceful place so you can choose a seat and rest for a while just observing that which is around you and drifting even deeper into the trance, with normal conscious awareness becoming more and more distant and your connection to this place stronger and stronger.

That which remains strong will be the sound of my voice; that you will always be able to hear and understand, so enjoy this experience and drift even deeper into the trance.

From this place you can go anywhere in space and time as you recognize and connect with your inner consciousness.

You may want to now visit your own place which can be a real memory or not, or stay here deeply relaxed in this safe place.

I don't know which place you might prefer but that doesn't matter because the place is your place and you can use it often to experience a peace and oneness with your being.

Suggestion

We all experience cycles in our energy systems of around 90 – 120 minutes that call for rest periods that modern lifestyles and work commitments don't allow for.

These Ultradian rhythms are, therefore often ignored, creating behavioral distortions such as bouts of tiredness, an increased desire to drink and some irritability, particularly if those desires aren't satisfied.

In a few moments you will be able to let your own subconscious mind address these questions in any way at all. No suggestion, no real direction from me, who, after all is an outsider in these matters, but just for you.

You will use the innate ability you already have to create new neural pathways and create new sets of synaptic connections to modify your behavior and achieve what you want.

It will be a kind of self re-programming exercise with no stimulus from the outside because a part of you will always fight against that. This is the rebellious subconscious at play.

The more that the outside tries to help or suggest or be involved the more it is resisted and that's ok, because that is a part of you and it makes you who you are.

So the time will be just for you.

Metaphor

Before that, though, you can assess how the troops line up. On the one hand there is your desire to be released from the need to drink and on the other all those pressures that make it so necessary.

They are opposing forces and in your wonderful imagination you can represent them facing each other in any way you want.

You might see them as opposing armies or tug-o-war teams or even contestants in a sporting contest or in any way at all.

Looking at these opposing forces you might well be able to assess who is the stronger right away, or you might not be entirely sure. It may be that the strength of the forces varies at times and advantage might shift from one to the other.

This isn't a fair contest though. It's not something you just have to observe and accept the outcome of because you have control over what happens and can influence the struggle to your advantage.

If they were opposing armies, for example, you might draft in reinforcements, or you might increase the potency of your side in some other way to ensure superiority.

So you can do that now.

Check the strength of your need to be free of alcohol, which we might call 'Team Me', against the desire to drink and we can call that one the 'Booze Team', then progressively or instantaneously add resources to 'Team Me' until it has superiority in all areas.

Make sure you are certain that 'Team Me' is stronger and when that is the case you can move on.

We will allow a few moments for this to complete so you can continue to relax and solidify that certainty that your need for alcohol will evaporate, it will just become less important and you may even dislike it.

Further metaphor

Now you can focus on restructuring your emotional centers using intention and visualization.

You might see the network as if it were a complex rail junction with interconnecting points everywhere. With just a thought you can shift any connection you might want to. So to begin with you might scan all of these junctions and select the ones that need to change.

There may be a number of emotional power sources maintaining connections to alcohol and drinking and as you find them you can disconnect the existing power source and install another one that moves the connection away from the unwanted behavior and installs a connection to a new healthy line.

You may see the unwanted connections as rusty, unmaintained and unsafe lines with weeds growing all around on rotten sleepers and all in all a dangerous way to go, whereas the route you want to follow has been newly constructed and is safe and well supported.

What is surprising and interesting about this is that as you move around in this metaphor, making the changes you want you will be altering the physical connections inside your brain.

Your thoughts will fire neurons and create synaptic pathways, those new connections just like the railway lines and in this manner you can embody and conjoin your mind and your brain to just change how you feel.

In a short time the music on the recording will end but you can finish when you are done before or after the recording completes.

Just know that you can do this and you can change and that you are in control of all of it.

Appendix 5

Alcoholics Anonymous 12 Steps

The original twelve steps (Alcoholics Anonymous)
We admitted we were powerless over alcohol—that our lives had become unmanageable.

Came to believe that a Power greater than ourselves could restore us to sanity.

Made a decision to turn our will and our lives over to the care of God as we understood Him.

Made a searching and fearless moral inventory of ourselves.

Admitted to God, to ourselves, and to another human being the exact nature of our wrongs.

Were entirely ready to have God remove all these defects of character.

Humbly asked Him to remove our shortcomings.

Made a list of all persons we had harmed, and became willing to make amends to them all.

Made direct amends to such people wherever possible, except when to do so would injure them or others.

Continued to take personal inventory and when we were wrong promptly admitted it.

Sought through prayer and meditation to improve our conscious contact with God as we understood Him, praying only for knowledge of His will for us and the power to carry that out.

Having had a spiritual awakening as the result of these steps, we tried to carry this message to alcoholics, and to practice these principles in all our affairs.

A revised/complimentary twelve steps (AA, 2002)
(Not formally considered to be within the 12 steps but an

addition to them for the organisers of each AA sub/regional group to employ as they wish)

Our common welfare should come first; personal recovery depends upon AA unity.

For our group purpose there is but one ultimate authority—a loving God as He may express Himself in our group conscience. Our leaders are but trusted servants; they do not govern.

The only requirement for AA membership is a desire to stop drinking.

Each group should be autonomous except in matters affecting other groups or AA as a whole.

Each group has but one primary purpose—to carry its message to the alcoholic who still suffers.

An AA group ought never endorse, finance, or lend the AA name to any related facility or outside enterprise, lest problems of money, property, and prestige divert us from our primary purpose.

Every AA group ought to be fully self-supporting, declining outside contributions.

Alcoholics Anonymous should remain forever non-professional, but our service centers may employ special workers.

AA, as such, ought never to be organized; but we may create service boards or committees directly responsible to those they serve.

Alcoholics Anonymous has no opinion on outside issues; hence the AA name ought never to be drawn into public controversy.

Our public relations policy is based on attraction rather than promotion; we need always maintain personal anonymity at the level of press, radio, and films.

Anonymity is the spiritual foundation of all our traditions, ever reminding us to place principles before personalities.

About the author

David Allen is first and foremost a family man. He has been married since 1969 and has two sons and five grandchildren. Family, stability and security play a large role in defining his perspective on life. He has a career background in engineering, management and marketing spanning over 40 years incorporating 15 years as an IT consultant. He has also been a keen sportsman, having played league cricket for 25 years and been actively involved with the British Karate Kyokushin organization for 20 years reaching the grade of 4th Dan though nowadays golf is his preferred activity. Prior to his involvement in the personal therapy arena he had had a number of different roles in both the sporting and the corporate world. This book benefits from a long and broad life experience.

He has advanced qualifications in both hypnotherapy and EFT and has been working as a therapist since 2004. His personal experience with alcohol underlies the motivation to help others with this most difficult of addictions. The message this book brings is typical of the searching, questioning intellect that drives him to seek solutions where conventional methodologies come up short. There are no sponsors and no vested interests underpinning this work. It stems from his personal client experience and benefits from an inherent freedom to question everything.

He runs his hypnotherapy practice in England and has also developed the world's first interactive online program to help people overcome their alcohol problems.

For more information visit David's websites at:

www.nlp-hypnotherapy.biz
www.control-your-drinking.co.uk
www.thesophisticatedalcoholic.com

End notes

1   World Centre for EFT. (n.d.). http://www.eftuniverse.com
2   The story is told in 'From Headlines to Hard Times' by Ed Mitchell. John Blake Publishing (2009 and 2010)
3   Alcoholics Anonymous. (n.d.). http://www.aa.org
4   Lipton, B. The Biology of Belief. Hay House; illustrated edition (September 15, 2008)
5   Watson, J.D, Crick, F. (1953). Molecular Structure of Nucleic Acids: A Structure for Deoxyribose Nucleic Acid
6   Wikipedia. (n.d.). http://en.wikipedia.org/wiki/Watson_and_Crick
7   Bruce H. Lipton., Steve Bhaerman Spontaneous Evolution, Hay House September 2009
8   Abate, T. (2001, February 11). http://articles.sfgate.com/2001-02-11/news/17583040_1_chemical-letters-president-of-celera-genomics-human-genome-project.
9   Richard Bandler, John Grinder. (1975). Patterns of the hypnotic techniques of Milton Erickson MD (Volume 1). Capitola: Meta Publications
10 Gary Craig, http://www.emofree.com/
11 Callahan, R. (n.d.). *http://www.rogercallahan.com/index2.php*
12 Wikipedia. (n.d.). *http://en.wikipedia.org/wiki/Acupuncture*
13 http://www.statistics.gov.uk/downloads/theme_health/CancerTrendsUpdates.pdf
14 John Diamond Life Energy: Using the Meridians to Unlock the Hidden Power of Your Emotions.   Paragon House; 1 edition (April 2, 1998)
15 http://www.statistics.gov.uk/pdfdir/alc0110.pdf
16 http://www.ias.org.uk/resources/factsheets/nhs.pdf
17 http://www.nhsconfed.org/Publications/briefings/Pages/

What-alcohol-costs-the-NHS.aspx
18 http://www.nhsconfed.org/Publications/briefings/Pages/
    What-alcohol-costs-the-NHS.aspx
19 http://www.ias.org.uk/resources/factsheets/health.pdf
20 http://www.ias.org.uk/resources/factsheets/advertising.pdf
21 http://en.Wikipedia.org/wiki/Carl_Jung
22 http://www.spiritualregression.org/
23 http://www.ias.org.uk/resources/factsheets/tax.pdf
24 National Institute for Health and Clinical Excellence. (2010).
    Alcohol-use disorders: preventing harmful drinking. NHS
25 www.drinkaware.co.uk, What did you drink yesterday?
    http://www.drinkaware.co.uk/tips-and-tools/drink-
    diary/?gclid=CKT55sPH7qYCFUEY4Qodx1n7HA

B O O K S

O is a symbol of the world, of oneness and unity. In different cultures it also means the "eye," symbolizing knowledge and insight. We aim to publish books that are accessible, constructive and that challenge accepted opinion, both that of academia and the "moral majority."

Our books are available in all good English language bookstores worldwide. If you don't see the book on the shelves ask the bookstore to order it for you, quoting the ISBN number and title. Alternatively you can order online (all major online retail sites carry our titles) or contact the distributor in the relevant country, listed on the copyright page.

See our website **www.o-books.net** for a full list of over 500 titles, growing by 100 a year.

And tune in to myspiritradio.com for our book review radio show, hosted by June-Elleni Laine, where you can listen to the authors discussing their books.

mySpiritRadio